Bearing the Word

Other titles in the 'Building Bridges' seminar series available from Church House Publishing

The Road Ahead: A Christian–Muslim Dialogue

Scriptures in Dialogue: Christians and Muslims studying the Bible and the Qur'ān together

Bearing the Word

Prophecy in Biblical and Qur'ānic perspective

A record of the third 'Building Bridges' seminar
held at Georgetown University, Washington DC,
30 March – 1 April 2004

Edited by Michael Ipgrave

CHURCH HOUSE PUBLISHING

Church House Publishing
Church House
Great Smith Street
London SW1P 3NZ

Tel: 020 7898 1451
Fax: 020 7898 1449

ISBN 0 7151 4050 7

Published 2005 by Church House Publishing

Cover design by Church House Publishing

Cover image: detail from a panel in the series 'Spirituality in the Wilderness' by Adam Boulter. Copyright © Adam Boulter 1999; reproduced by kind permission of the artist and St Hugh's (Charterhouse-in-Southwark), Bermondsey.

Typeset by RefineCatch Limited, Bungay, Suffolk
Printed in England by The Cromwell Press Ltd, Trowbridge, Wiltshire

Contents

Participants vii

Introduction Building Bridges in Georgetown xi

Chapter 1 What is dialogue? 1

Analysing atheism: Unbelief and the world of faiths 1
Rowan Williams

Scriptures in dialogue: Are we reckoning without the host? 13
Mustansir Mir

Hospitable readings: Comments on *Scriptures in Dialogue* 20
Miroslav Volf

Chapter 2 Called by God 29

Scripture dialogue I 29
Ṭā Hā 20.1-36; Exodus 3.1-14

Scripture dialogue II 36
Acts 9.1-22; *al-Muzzammil* 73.1-20

Questions from the scriptures 43

Chapter 3 What is prophecy? 45

What is prophecy? Reflections on a Qur'ānic institution in history 45
Wadad Kadi

'My devoted friend': The prophet as the intimate of God 59
Ellen F. Davis

Chapter 4 Sent to humanity 67

Scripture dialogue III 67
Hūd 11.25-49; Jeremiah 26

Scripture dialogue IV 76
1 Kings 21; *al-Shu'arā'* 26.123-91

Questions from the scriptures 85

Chapter 5 Jesus and Muhammad 87

'Īsā and Jesus: Christ in Islamic Christology 87
Mahmoud Ayoub

Jesus and Muhammad: The sufficiency of prophecy 90
Daniel Madigan

Chapter 6 The completion of prophecy 100

Scripture dialogue V 100
Maryam 19.16-36; Luke 1.26-38

Scripture dialogue VI 107
Hebrews 1.1-4; *al-Aḥzāb* 33.40, *al-Mā'ida* 5.3

Questions from the scriptures 113

Chapter 7 Reflections from the dialogue 116

Building bridges: A personal reflection from a Christian 116
Teresa Okure

Bearing the Word: Prophecy in Christian and Islamic scriptures 124
Michael Ipgrave

Notes 141

Participants

Professor Muhammad Abdel Haleem
King Fahd Professor of Islamic Studies, School of Oriental and African Studies, University of London

Monsignor Khaled Akasheh
Head Office for Islam, Pontifical Council for Interreligious Dialogue, Vatican City

Dr Mahmoud Ayoub
Professor of Islamic Studies and Comparative Religion, Temple University, Philadelphia

Professor Azyumardi Azra
Professor of History and Rector, State Islamic University, Indonesia

Sheikh Dr M. A. Zaki Badawi
Principal, The Muslim College, London

Professor Vincent Cornell
Director, King Fahd Center for Middle East and Islamic Studies, University of Arkansas

Professor Ahmad Dallal
Chairman, Department of Arabic Language, Literature and Linguistics, Georgetown University

Professor Ellen F. Davis
Professor of Bible and Practical Theology, Duke University, Durham, North Carolina

Professor John L. Esposito
Professor of Religion and International Affairs and of Islamic Studies, Director of the Center for Muslim–Christian Understanding, Georgetown University

Dr Ida Glaser
Senior Teaching and Research Fellow, Edinburgh Centre for Muslim-Christian Studies

The Revd Canon Dr Michael Ipgrave
Inter Faith Relations Adviser, Archbishops' Council of the Church of England

Professor Wadad Kadi
Professor of Islamic Thought, Department of Near Eastern Languages and Civilizations, University of Chicago

Dr Hashim Kamali
Professor of Law, International Islamic University, Malaysia

Dr Enes Karic
Professor of Qur'anic Studies, Faculty of Islamic Studies, Sarajevo

The Revd Professor John Langan SJ
Joseph Cardinal Bernardin Professor of Catholic Social Thought, Georgetown University

Professor Jane Dammen McAuliffe
Dean of the College and Professor in the Department of Arabic, Georgetown University

The Revd Dr Daniel Madigan SJ
Director, Institute for the Study of Religions and Cultures, Pontifical Gregorian University, Rome

Professor Mustansir Mir
University Professor of Islamic Studies, Youngstown State University, Ohio

Dr Tarek Mitri
Coordinator, Inter-Religious Relations, World Council of Churches, Geneva

Dr Aref Nayed
Visiting Fellow, The Centre for Advanced Religious and Theological Studies, Faculty of Divinity, Cambridge University

The Rt Revd Dr Michael Nazir-Ali
Bishop of Rochester

The Revd Sr Professor Dr Teresa Okure SHCJ
Head of Department of Biblical Studies, Catholic Institute of West Africa, Nigeria

Dr Mona Siddiqui
Senior Lecturer in Arabic and Islamic Studies and Head of Department of Theology and Religious Studies, University of Glasgow

Professor Miroslav Volf
Henry B. Wright Professor of Theology, Yale University Divinity School

Professor John O. Voll
Professor of Islamic History and Associate Director, Center for Muslim–Christian Understanding, Georgetown University

The Most Revd and Rt Hon. Dr Rowan Williams
Archbishop of Canterbury

Mr Timothy Winter
Lecturer in Islamic Studies, Faculty of Divinity, Cambridge University

Dr Ishtiyaq Ahmad Zilli
Professor, Department of History, Aligarh Muslim University, India

Monsignor Mato Zovkić
Vicar General of the Archdiocese of Sarajevo

Introduction

Building Bridges in Georgetown

This book provides a record of, and a reflection on, the third 'Building Bridges' seminar of Christians and Muslims,[1] convened by the Archbishop of Canterbury, and hosted by Georgetown University, Washington from 30 March to 1 April 2004. The seminar involved thirty Christian and Muslim scholars from around the world, and included public lectures, group scripture studies and plenary discussions. The focus of the dialogue on this occasion was on 'prophecy' in its biblical and Qur'ānic forms.

The material presented here includes the texts of the lectures delivered during the seminar, an account of the dialogues between the scriptural texts in which participants engaged in small groups, and two reflections on the dialogue as a whole. The scriptural material is arranged in three chapters, corresponding to the three days of the seminar's study. Each chapter comprises two pairs of scriptures – a biblical and a Qur'ānic passage were studied together in the groups. For each passage, an English translation of the text is followed by a brief general commentary and by more detailed notes; these reflect the conversations held within the groups, while clearly not being able to pick up every point made. Each of the chapters of scriptural dialogue concludes by suggesting some further questions which face Muslims and Christians as they read these texts together.

Biblical quotations are according to the New Revised Standard Version, except where otherwise indicated. The texts used for the Qur'ān are from the new translation by Professor Muhammad Abdel Haleem,[2] who was himself one of the seminar participants. I am grateful to him for permission to use his translation, and to the Revd Canon Dr David Marshall for reading through this text and making many helpful suggestions. Thanks are also due to all the participants who provided reports of discussions in their groups, and to those who supplied introductory material for the various texts or who contributed reflections later. While the book does try to capture the discussions of the seminar, the reportage inevitably reflects my own perspectives, and in the last reflection I have unashamedly woven the many insights of participants together with my own thoughts. Clearly, this means that I take full responsibility for the errors or misrepresentations which doubtless abound in these pages.

Chapter 1

What is dialogue?

Before engaging in the shared reading and discussion of scriptural texts, participants in the seminar had opportunities to think about the meaning and the presuppositions of dialogue. Archbishop Rowan Williams's lecture – delivered in Georgetown University the night before the seminar opened – explores the idea of dialogue as an encounter of different disbeliefs, suggesting that our different faiths can be purified and strengthened by the challenges of understanding what the other does not believe in, just as religious faith can be purified and strengthened by the challenge of atheism. Mustansir Mir, asking about the scriptural basis of inter faith dialogue for Muslims, sharply questions the interpretation commonly given to some Qur'ānic verses. He urges that, rather than pressing individual texts into service in dubious ways to validate interreligious cooperation, what is needed is a 'post-prophetic' theology based on a reading of the Qur'ān as a whole. Miroslav Volf offers some reflections on the preceding 'Building Bridges' seminar, held in Qatar in 2003, and more generally on the method of 'scriptures in dialogue'. He argues that, because the Qur'ān and the Bible are so formative for Muslims and Christians, engaging with one another's scriptures brings us to the very heart of who we are as people of faith, and opens up a door of 'interpretive hospitality', inviting us to understand better and appreciate more the other in their otherness.

Analysing atheism: Unbelief and the world of faiths

Rowan Williams

In the year 156 of the Christian era, Polycarp, Bishop of Smyrna, was arrested and brought before the magistrate, charged with being a Christian. He was in his eighties, and his age and frailty prompted the magistrate to offer him a quick discharge if he would acknowledge the divine spirit of the emperor and say 'Away with the atheists.' The latter, at least, you might think would not be difficult for a bishop; but of course at this period an atheist was someone who refused to take part in the civic cult of the empire, to perform public religious duties and take part in the festivals of the Roman city. Christians were atheists, by this definition; Polycarp had a problem after all. His response, though, was an elegant turning of the tables. He looked around slowly at the screaming mob in the amphitheatre which had gathered for the gladiatorial fights and public executions, and, says our eyewitness chronicler, he groaned and said, 'Away with the atheists.'

The magistrate did not fail to grasp the theological point, and Polycarp was duly condemned to be burned alive. But this poignant story is one well worth pondering for reasons beyond the study of early Christianity. It is a reminder that 'atheism' may be a less simple idea than either its defenders or its attackers assume. People often talk as though 'atheism' were a self-contained system, a view of the world which gained its coherence from a central conviction – that there is no transcendent creative power independent of the universe we experience. But the story of Polycarp reminds us that to understand what atheism means we need to know which gods are being rejected and why.

Thus an early Christian was an atheist because he or she refused to be part of a complex system in which political and religious loyalties were inseparably bound up. 'Atheism' was a decision to place certain loyalties above those owed to the sacralized power of the state. But, moving across the world of faiths, Buddhists are sometimes described as atheists by puzzled observers, aware of the fact that Buddhist philosophy has no place for a divine agent and that Buddhist practice concentrates exclusively upon the mind purifying itself from self-absorption and craving; here, 'atheism' is a strategy to discipline the mind's temptation to distraction by speculative thought. Whether or not there is a transcendent creator is irrelevant to the mind's work; preoccupation with this is a self-indulgent diversion at best, and at worst a search for some agency that can do the work only we can do.

Neither of these has much in common with the atheism characteristic of Western modernity, which draws much of its energy from moral protest. The God of Jewish and Christian faith is seen as an agent who has the power to prevent the world's evil yet refuses to do so, so that there is the appearance of a moral incoherence at the heart of this tradition. Or he is seen as an arbitrary tyrant whose will is inimical to the liberty of human creatures; or else as an impotent and remote reality, a concept given a sort of ghostly existence by human imagination. In all these instances, it is clear that the refusal of belief in God is something essential to human liberation. We cannot live with a God who is responsible for evil; we cannot grow up as human beings if what is demanded of us is blind obedience; we cannot mortgage our lives and our loving commitment to an animated abstraction. Atheism here is necessary to maturity, individually and culturally.

Even those who argue at length about the simply conceptual inadequacies, as they see it, of Western religion – classically, writers in the Bertrand Russell style – will frequently deploy the language of moral revolt as well. 'Protest atheism', as it is often called, has become a familiar element in the armoury of modern intellectual life, perhaps more often repeated than expounded, but culturally very powerful. The more austere objection to belief found in the positivism of the early to mid-twentieth century – it is equally without meaning to affirm or to deny the existence of an agency whose existence could never be empirically demonstrated – has an ironic resonance with Buddhism, but is another component in the mind of Western modernity, even when the philosophical system from which it arises no longer has much credibility. This is atheism as the mark of supreme intellectual detachment, with the intellect defined as a mechanism for processing checkable information only, with everything else reduced to emotive noise. But the other great modern version of atheism is that which exposes religious talk as ideological – as an instrument of social control whose surface conceptual structure is designed to obscure its real function and to divert thought, emotion and energy from real to unreal objects. This is the essence of Marxist atheism, but it also has some relation to Nietzsche's unforgettably eloquent polemic against Christian faith.

The point is that atheism is to be defined as a system only by some dramatic intellectual contortions. A number of intellectual and spiritual policies involve or at least accompany the denial of certain versions of the divine, especially the divine as an active and intelligent subject; but in each case the denial is not intelligible apart from a specific context of thought and image, representation and misrepresentation of specific religious doctrines, and the overall system of which the denial is a part is not necessarily shaped by it. This is why the recent proposal in the United Kingdom that religious education in schools should give attention to 'atheism and humanism' as 'non-faith belief systems' alongside the traditional religions was based on some serious conceptual confusions and category mistakes. In the background is the pervasive assumption of modernity that the intellectual default position is non-religious; but what this fails to see is that non-religiousness is historically and culturally a complex of refusals directed at specific religious doctrines, rather than a pure and primitive vision invaded by religious fictions. And if this is so, either religious education has to locate non-religious positions in relation to what it is that they deny, or it will end up treating atheism as the only position not subject to critical scrutiny and the construction of a proper intellectual genealogy: not a welcome position for a rationalist to be in.

In fact the incorporation of critical positions into religious education is to be applauded. To see where the points of strain are to be found in a religious discourse and to seek to understand how a thoughtful and self-critical tradition can respond to them is essential to a proper grasp of religious identities. One of the weaknesses of the kind of religious education now common in schools (in the United Kingdom at least) is that it tends to describe the positions of faith communities as finished systems for which questions have been answered rather than (to borrow Alasdair Macintyre's phrase) 'continuities of conflict',[1] in which the moral, spiritual and intellectual tensions constantly press believers towards a fuller, more comprehensive statement of their commitments.

'If you meet the Buddha, kill him' is a well-known Zen dictum, from a tradition deeply aware that personal agenda and history are easily capable of distorting any supposedly clear vision of where enlightenment is to be found. Any conceptual form that can be given in the abstract to the Buddha (i.e. to the enlightened awareness) will take its shape from the unenlightened awareness, and so has to be dissolved. But this is not that different from the conviction of much Hindu thought, that the divine is 'not this, not that', never identifiable with a determinate object, or from the principle, deeply rooted in the Abrahamic faiths, that God cannot be given an 'essential' definition, classified as a kind of object. This may be expressed in the form of the apophatic theology of an Ibn Sina or Maimonides or Nicholas of Cusa: Ibn Sina (like Aquinas and all that flows from him) insists that there can be no answer to the question, 'What makes God divine?' as if some 'quiddity' could be identified that grounded a divine definition. God is God by being God – by being the necessary, uncaused active reality he is; nothing else. But the same point is made in wholly different idioms by twentieth-century writers such as Karl Barth and Simone Weil. For Barth, all systems for which God is an object are unsustainable: he always speaks before we have words to answer, acts before we can locate him on some intellectual map. He is never 'available', though always present. And Simone Weil, in an argument of some complexity, concludes that when the human ego says 'God', it cannot be referring to any reality to which the name might be truthfully applied. Because the 'I' that says 'God' is always self-directed and so wedded to untruth, God cannot properly be spoken of. Any God my selfish mind can conceive is bound to be a false, non-existent God. The true God is known only in ways that cannot be reduced to theory or third-person language. If you meet God (in the language of systematic theology or metaphysics), kill him.

It seems that, in differing degrees, most major religious discourses require and cultivate unbelief – that is, unbelief in a divine agent who can be thought about as an agent among others, an instance of a type, a kind of life that can be defined in terms of something other or prior. Thus when we try to consider and understand atheism of any kind, our first question has to be what it is about some particular piece of speech about God is causing trouble, and whether it is in fact essential to a religious tradition's understanding of what it means by God or the divine. It may be, of course, that what is objected to really is what a religious tradition believes; but even if it is, it is crucial to explore where the points of strain are felt, so that convictions may be tested and if possible reinforced. So the challenge of atheism in its various guises is one that has the potential to deepen what is said about our commitments; not for nothing did Olivier Clément, the French Orthodox theologian, write about 'purification by atheism'. To come to the point where you disbelieve passionately in a certain kind of God may be the most important step you can take in the direction of the true God.

But what I want to suggest specifically in connection with the dialogue between the world faiths is that we spend more time looking at what is disbelieved in other religious discourses. A few years ago, an American theologian wrote a book[2] about Christian doctrine as a series of 'unbeliefs': what does Christianity commit you to denying about God and Christ? I wonder if the same method might not be illuminating as we look across the faiths. Just as in the case of atheism generally we learn what we are and are not really committed to, so in dialogue or trialogue or whatever between faiths, we might be able to learn from each other's disbeliefs, to be 'purified' by encountering and examining the protests and denials, the 'atheisms', of each other's views.

Let me try to illustrate; I shall concentrate chiefly upon the Abrahamic faiths, but it should be clear at the very start of this reflection that Buddhism is of special significance in its denial of any personal agency outside the bounds of the world. If we ask why such a denial is made, we must conclude, as suggested earlier, that there is an anxiety that projection on to an external deity fatally weakens the incentive to dealing with our own distraction and selfishness; and there is an anxiety that the very act of affirming the existence of such a deity constitutes an escape from the severely practical analysis of the mind's liberation. In response to this, all three of the Abrahamic faiths have to examine themselves carefully. If we believe in a source of energy, forgiveness and love independent of ourselves, how exactly do we prevent it from becoming a belief that weakens our responsibility and imprisons us in fantasy? We shall need (to say no more in detail) to establish that we are not looking for a supernatural agent to fill the gaps in our imperfect self-awareness and willingness to change, a consoling personality who is there to serve the needs of our idle and needy selves. We shall need to examine carefully those aspects of our language which themselves warn against just such a misunderstanding – and those which might most easily suggest it or nourish it. Our faith becomes self-aware in a fresh way; even if we end by saying – as we probably shall – that the Buddhist refusal of a personal God assumes that ascribing personality and objectivity to God must always be a simple projection of our need, and if we argue – as we probably shall – that nothing is served by denying the fact of our dependence on what lies beyond the world, we shall have been warned, sharply and constructively, of just how we may use our faith to reinforce what is least converted in us.

But how might this apply to the conversation between the Abrahamic traditions? Here are some suggestions.

The Jew disbelieves propositions like the following: God is free to disregard or rewrite the solemn promise made to a specific people at a point in history; God makes no specific demands on those God chooses to hold in the closeness consequent upon such a promise; God cannot deal adequately with the world by revealing the divine will, but has to intervene in allegedly more 'intimate' or direct ways.

The Christian disbelieves propositions like these: God needs to be persuaded by our virtue to love us or to act on our behalf; God is a solitary individual with a personality comparable to that of a human individual; God is metaphysically incapable of acting in and as a created and dependent being; God's action can have no impact upon physical processes.

And the Muslim disbelieves propositions like these: God is the compound of several distinct divine agents (whether an indeterminate number or just three); God wills that the divine purpose be realized only in the lives of a limited segment of society or humanity; God's will can be divorced from the supposed cultural limitations of its earliest definitive and complete expression; God is known by a complex of human approximations to truth.

As will be evident, there is overlap in these configurations; and all three traditions agree in disbelieving in a God who is one of the items that exists within the universe, who is subject to time and change as finite beings are, who shares the same conceptual territory as do the limited agents we are familiar with. Although Christianity and Judaism have increasingly been willing to entertain images suggesting vulnerability and suffering in the divine life, this is largely a modern development whose conceptual relation to the definitive doctrines of the religions is a rather uneasy business. Powerful devotional metaphors require careful handling in this context, and they should not obscure one of the most significant convergences that exists between the Abrahamic faiths – and indeed between these faiths and others – on the conviction that God is not a member of any class of existent beings. You will recall the earlier reference to Ibn Sina, echoed to the letter by Aquinas.

That being said, however, the respective systems of disbelief I have sketched so briefly pose equally significant mutual challenges. Faced with the disbeliefs of another discourse, each of the three participants in the Abrahamic conversation should be prompted to ask whether the God of the other's disbelief is or is not the God they themselves believe in. If the answer were a simple yes, dialogue might be a great deal more difficult than it is; the reality of dialogue suggests that we do not in fact have to do with a simple 'atheism' in respect of the other's models of God. And part of the fascination and the spiritual significance of dialogue is the discovery of how one's own commitments actually work, and specifically how they work under pressure. Is Christianity that which Judaism as such denies? Is the affirmation of Christianity identical to the denial of what Jews believe as Jews? And so with Islam also; one of the darkest and most tragic parts of our history in relation to other faiths ('our' history being, for these purposes, the history of all the Abrahamic faiths) is the construction of the other as the opposite. To pick up an idea which I have tried to develop elsewhere, we have to put behind us a picture of the world of faiths in which each is seen as answering the same questions, so that the respective 'performance' of different traditions can be categorized in terms of right and wrong answers to these questions. Binary oppositions do not serve us at all here.

So to some of the particulars, though we can only take a few examples. I begin with two Muslim disbeliefs and their impact on Christian–Muslim encounter. The Muslim disbelieves in a plurality of divine agents: so the Christian has to ask whether his or her belief is properly so characterized – and if it is not, to examine why and how it could come to be read that way. Thus the Christian may say, in the tradition of Augustine and Aquinas, that belief in the Trinity is not belief in three self-subsisting individuals sharing a divine nature; it is to claim that the life that is divine life exists as three utterly interdependent 'streams' of agency, which cannot be reduced to each other – an originating agency, a responsive agency, an excess of creative and eternal agency always free to replicate the pattern of origin and response. The Greek tradition avoids calling them 'persons' and prefers 'subsistents' (*hupostaseis*). This is a very abstract rendering indeed of the doctrine of the Trinity, but one which avoids the distorting impression that Christians believe in some kind of divine society of individuals; and there are aspects of both theology and popular devotion that can give such an impression of a belief which Muslims (and Jews) find incomprehensible and inconsistent with belief in the oneness of God. The important clarification for the Christian is that divine oneness is not the oneness of an individual (where there may logically be more than one of its kind) – and this is actually something that can be agreed by the Jew and the Muslim, who (at least in the shape of their mainstream philosophical systems) would equally deny that God is an individual in that sense. The Muslim challenge pushes the Christian, now as in the Middle Ages, to clarify a fundamental point of belief.

Imagine, next, the Christian picking up a Muslim unbelief and challenging it. The Muslim does not believe in a 'Church' that is socially a separate body from the political community at large as organized by divine law. The Christian however has a long tradition of expecting the body of believers to be in significant respects different from political society (think of Polycarp again). Is the Muslim attitude not tantamount to saying that nothing but a theocracy can express Islam? To which the Muslim might respond by saying that if God is a God who has the capacity to make known the divine will, and if there is ultimately one good for human society which is to be found in following that will, there can be no stability or justice in a society that is not founded upon revealed law. But this does not at all mean that 'religious' authorities must dominate the state, or that the free exercise of different faiths is unthinkable. First, there are no simply religious authorities in the Western and Christian sense: there is a community (a political community, naturally, since that is how communities organize themselves) of those who have willingly submitted to revealed law. Second, only free submission to God's law is a proper foundation for the 'House of Islam': it may be necessary to combat the unbeliever as a political assailant, but this is not to deny the liberty in principle of any human being to be subject to God or not. Even the issue of voluntary abandonment of Islam is a subject that needs to be looked at with nuance; this is by definition a political offence, yet it is not wholly clear in Muslim jurisprudence that it merits an extreme political penalty. But the Muslim might emerge from the discussion conscious of a question about why and how the Christian might see this as a denial of human liberty; and the upshot could be a deeper recognition of the logic of free submission, and the unavoidably paradoxical nature of a political community governed by law which also assumes that loyalty and obedience to this community cannot be secured by external sanctions that seek to constrain the will by threat. And so the Muslim, challenged about a disbelief by the Christian, is taken back to the most fundamental defining question of Islam, the character of obedience.

Is what the Muslim denies what the Christian affirms? It seems less obvious than at the beginning of the argument. The Muslim is not a theocrat as the Christian West might understand the term: the denial of a 'secular' space is not a claim to impose religious authority over some other kind, but the acknowledgement that only one basis exists for coherent political life of any kind. The Christian may in fact agree; but will argue that in the realities of a historical existence where levels of submission to God are varied (to say the least), there is bound to be a tension between the community which lives professedly by God's law and the turbulent and unstable succession of social orders which arise in turn around it. Dealing with the Muslim's refusal of belief in any 'Church-like' body, existing as a distinct entity within civil society, may clarify both the Muslim's view of freedom and obedience and the Christian's eschatological reserve about any historical political order. And as in my first instance, a language for the conversation appears as this clarification advances, a language about God's will to be known and the necessity of such knowledge for a social life free from incoherent rivalry and struggle and injustice.

So to the disbelief of the Jew. Both Christian and Muslim apparently hold that God is at liberty to revise the divine promises; and in such a God the Jew cannot believe. A God who changed his mind would be precisely a God whose freedom would be subject to limit and negotiation, a God whose word once spoken could be rescinded. Hebrew scripture explicitly rules out such a thought, and Jewish philosophy understandably regards the mutability of divine election as diminishing God. Is this a fair perception of the God of Muslims and Christians? The Christian, of course, has the entire argument of Christian scripture to appeal to, especially the complex arguments of Paul in Romans. The promise is made to Abraham's children, but God has extended the definition to include those who become Abraham's children by imitating his faith not simply by lineage; thus those who enter the Christian Church are honorary or adoptive Jews. God is faithful – a point insisted upon by Paul against those who would indeed argue that God's mind has changed and the Jewish people are rejected. The Muslim will go back to the story of Abraham in the Qur'ān, accepting that there is a history of some sort of covenant (though with Ishmael as well as Isaac); but what constitutes covenantal obligation on the human side is that obedience which is now given final form in Muslim revelation, of which all earlier prophecy and theophany is a foreshadowing.

Neither Christian nor Muslim believes in a mutable God; but both will be properly challenged by the Jew to look at the coherence of their own stories, especially in the light of the persistence of Jewish religion and nationality. The question about God becomes intimately associated with a question about power. If the Christian and the Muslim are incorporating Jewish history into their narrative, does the Jew have the right to speak for himself or herself, and to be heard? Jewish disbelief in a changeable God is linked (in a way that does not apply to Christians and Muslims) with Jewish self-belief, the confidence of the Jewish people that they are immutably a people. If Christian and Muslim theologies, even when they confess an immutable God, presuppose the mutability of Jewish identity or legitimacy, they claim a very specific kind of power, a power to declare someone else's history over. Jewish disbelief challenges at the deepest level the way such claims may and do emerge in the histories of the younger faiths. Can Christianity and Islam sustain themselves against the accusation of promoting a theological imperialism which has, from a Jewish point of view, nakedly and often murderously political implications?

And once again, there are answers that may emerge. Christians (Christians other than the extreme dispensationalist Christian

Zionists anyway) will often find difficulty in offering a theologically positive valuation of the continuing identity of the Jewish people, but may still believe that it is necessary to work at this, if only in terms of the people of Israel as the radical sign of the Church's incompleteness and the priority of the covenant people into whom non-Jews are now believed to be incorporated. The Muslim – paradoxically, more than the Christian in some respects – has a powerful sense of a shared prophetic history, but is unlikely to compromise over the supersession of Torah by Qur'ān. Yet the Muslim will also understand the inseparability of law and people in ways that a Christian might find harder, since it bears a certain similarity to the Muslim denial of neutral secularity and of a separated religious society; hence the often exemplary record of Muslim toleration of Jews as a nation within the nation.

Many other comparable exercises could be carried out in respect of the impact of 'disbeliefs' upon dialogue between the Abrahamic faiths, but I hope that the point of the discussion may be emerging. I am proposing that there is some analogy between the significance of particular unbeliefs upon the self-understanding of religious discourse in general and the significance of the 'unbeliefs' of particular religious discourses for each other. There is no such thing as a global system of 'atheism': there are denials of specific doctrines on varying grounds, and the examination of where the points of stress are in the exposition of these doctrines very importantly allows us to test the resources of what we say as believers – and, ideally, to emerge with a more robust sense of those resources. But equally, conversation between faith traditions can sometimes give the impression that part of the essence of one religious idiom is its disbelief in the God supposedly revealed in another; so that binary oppositions dominate our attitudes. Treat these disbeliefs, I am suggesting, as we might imaginatively and sensitively treat atheism; that is, try to see why what is denied is denied, and whether that denial is directed against what another tradition in fact claims. And in the light of that, try to discover what your own tradition commits you to and how it answers legitimate criticism from outside – criticism which often (as in the case of the mutability of God) could be raised intelligibly within the native tradition. What emerges is frequently a conceptual and imaginative world in which at least some of the positive concerns of diverse traditions are seen to be held in common.

But this is not at all to condemn inter faith dialogue to the sterile and abstract task so often envisaged for it, of identifying a common core of beliefs. The exercise I have been describing is not about finding a common core at all; it is about finding the appropriate language in which difference can be talked about rather than used as an excuse for violent separation. Just as in an encounter with atheists, it is sometimes possible to grasp the positive sense or expectation that leads an atheist to reject what he or she imagines is God, so that the conversation does not simply end in the positing of affirmation and denial, so here. We should certainly not be looking for a common core of belief between believer and atheist, but for a language in which to acknowledge and understand the difference. And in inter faith conversation, we continue to make the claims we make out of conviction of the truth, but seek to break through the assumption that everything can be reduced to whether people say yes or no to a set of simple propositions. Only in the wake of such a move can true dialogue proceed; it does not in fact happen when the 'common core' model is at work, because the hidden assumption is that what is common is bound to be what matters – in which case, difference is not really interesting, intellectually or spiritually. Nor does it happen when the relation between the faiths is seen as one between a set of correct answers and several sets of incorrect ones.

This lecture began as a reflection on the slippery character of the word 'atheism', and the need to resist the elevation of atheism to the level of a system – a danger which has been very publicly around in educational debates in the United Kingdom in recent months. But the more we recognize the variegated sense of atheism, the more important it may appear to approach the denials made by atheists as a way into understanding more thoroughly what doctrines and commitments do and do not entail. And on the basis of this, we have moved on to look at the denials, the unbeliefs of certain religious traditions, denials often assumed (both within and beyond a tradition) to be necessarily connected with the refusal of the truth of another faith, seen as a system constructed on the basis of what one tradition or another denies. To allow atheistic schemes to be examined as more than just the elaboration of a single denial, and to allow religious faiths to be examined as more than a map of mutual exclusions and incompatibilities, are closely connected exercises. Hence the suggestion, not after all so paradoxical, that we can learn better how to understand other religious believers if we learn better how to understand unbelievers. If both enterprises lead us back to an enhanced appreciation of the resource and complexity which our own faith both offers us and demands of us, so that we are more and not less confident in dialogue, we shall not have wasted our time.

Scriptures in dialogue: Are we reckoning without the host?

Mustansir Mir

The word 'dialogue' enjoys a certain respectability; it signifies a readiness to listen as well as to speak. As such, it connotes a welcome congeniality of atmosphere and holds out the promise of compromise and understanding. It seems right and proper to promote dialogue and engage in it and wrong and improper to oppose or undermine it. Dialogue based on scripture has an added halo. Whoever would think of questioning the advisability of such dialogue, especially today, when the need for understanding among the world's religious – more specifically, theistic – communities is said to be so great? Yet, I am going to take the inexpedient route of raising a few questions with regard to the very possibility of scripture-based dialogue. I intend to ask, with reference to the Qur'ān, whether we have sufficient scriptural warrant to hold such dialogue. I do not cast myself in the role of the stinging bee of Athens – that would be too great an honour to claim; but I do not see myself as a fly in the ointment either. I do mean to be very straightforward, or 'up front', though. Some of the statements I am going to make might sound provocative, anarchic, even seditious. But my intentions in undertaking the present exercise are, I assure you, much more honest than those of Brutus; and I do not wish to say, in concert with the inspired Plebeians of Rome, 'About! Seek! Burn! Fire! Kill! Slay!'

This presentation, I should emphasize, consists of personal reflections. It is not a research paper. An ideal research paper, of course, is one in which the author first writes the footnotes and then provides a matching text. I have not tried to write such a paper. Avoiding convoluted argument and without going too far afield, I will address two simple questions within the context of this seminar:

1. Does the Qur'ān allow dialogue with the People of the Book, that is, Jews and Christians?
2. If it allows such dialogue, then under what conditions does it allow it? If it does not allow such dialogue, then what are we doing here – or, more to the point – what am I doing here?

I am going to argue that the case usually based on the Qur'ān for interreligious dialogue is not very strong. I will then present my own position on the subject.

Even a cursory reading of the Qur'ān will leave one with the unmistakable impression that it is marked by a very high degree of self-assurance. At no point does the Qur'ān suffer from self-doubt. It says that it is free of all doubt (*lā rayba fīhi*);[3] that it represents the truth (*ḥaqq*);[4] that it is criterial in character (*furqān*);[5] that it has been sent down to settle disputes.[6] The Qur'ān invites people to accept it as the Word of God and challenges those who dismiss it as a human product to produce the like of it.[7] It establishes two diametrically opposed camps, one of *mu'minūn*, or believers, and the other of *kāfirūn*, or disbelievers (I am deliberately using the word 'disbelievers' instead of the palliative but less accurate 'unbelievers' or 'non-believers'). The Qur'ān gives good tidings to those who believe in it and gives dire warnings to those who deny it. It rejects the possibility of any compromise between *ḥaqq* and *bāṭil*, saying *fa-mā dhā ba'da l-ḥaqqi illa ḍ-ḍalāl* ('And what is left there after the truth except misguidance?').[8] It relentlessly criticizes those who row simultaneously in the two boats of *ḥaqq* and *bāṭil* and calls them *munāfiqūn*, or hypocrites,[9] and says that the *munāfiqūn* will occupy the lowest region of hell in the hereafter.[10] Bluntly unequivocal about the validity of its message, the Qur'ān seems to leave little choice to those whom it addresses: believe or else.

If I have already ruffled some feathers, then this is an indication that I am doing well. But there is more to come. Until now, I have talked in general terms. I will now examine a few specific Qur'ānic verses that are often cited to prove that the Qur'ān is all for interreligious dialogue. One very popular such verse is translated by Arberry as follows:

> Surely they that believe, and those of Jewry, and the Christians, and those Sabaeans, whoso believes in God and the Last Day, and works righteousness – their wage awaits them with their Lord, and no fear shall be on them, neither shall they sorrow.[11]

This verse is taken to be the Qur'ānic *magna carta* of religious diversity and religious dialogue. It is interpreted to mean that belief in God, belief in the afterlife, and good works are sufficient for salvation irrespective of whether such belief and works belong in Islam, in Judaism, in Christianity, or in Sabaeanism – or, by extension, in other religions.

This interpretation is vulnerable on more grounds than one. First, does the verse mean that, in the realm of belief, it is unnecessary to believe in prophets and scriptures? And does it mean, in the realm of action, that the Qur'ān does not care to define the substance of 'righteousness' and would approve of any works as long as they were defined by anyone in any sense as 'righteous'?

Second, taken in context, the verse would appear to have a meaning exactly opposite to the one that is thought to support the notion of religious rapprochement. The entire passage preceding the verse[12] is in criticism of Jews, citing as it does such incidents in Jewish history as the worship of the calf and the demand for seeing God with human eyes. The verses immediately following are no less critical. It is hard to believe that this one verse is subversive of this larger, through-and-through critical statement. Quite in line with the content of the larger section of which it is a part, it says that the Jews – or the followers of any other religion, for that matter – should not take their salvation for granted, for salvation depends not on association with or membership in a certain group but on correct belief and proper conduct. It goes without saying that one will have to read the whole of the Qur'ān to determine what the Qur'ān regards as correct belief and proper conduct.

Third, if the Qur'ān were to allow for multiple repositories of truth, then the entire project of the Qur'ān would become an exercise in futility. If not only Islam but other religions are equally valid paths to salvation, then one wonders why the Qur'ān is, at times, severely critical of the People of the Book and why it emphasizes that it is necessary for the People of the Book to believe in Muhammad and the Qur'ān.[13]

The second verse I would like to look at is this:

> Say: 'People of the Book! Come now to a word common between us and you, that we serve none but God, and that we associate not aught with Him, and do not some of us take others as Lords, apart from God.' And if they turn their backs, say: 'Bear witness that we are Muslims.'[14]

The verse's invitation to the People of the Book to 'come to a word common between us and you' – that is, between Muslims and Christians – is said to furnish grounds for inter faith dialogue. This is highly doubtful. Like *al-Baqara* 2.62, which occurs in a context of exclusivist Jewish–Muslim debate, *Āl 'Imrān* 3.64, too, is part of an exclusivist Christian–Muslim debate. The verses preceding and following it offer a serious indictment of the People of the Book.[15] Specifically, the Christians are told that deification of Jesus is unjustified since Adam, who was born without either parent, would be the more deserving of deification if birth without a father were to be taken as grounds for deifying Jesus.[16] *Āl 'Imrān* 3.61 records the incident of *ibtihāl*, or mutual cursing, to which the visiting Christian delegation from Najrān was invited. It is true that the members of the delegation had been put up at the Prophet's mosque in Madinah and the Prophet had allowed them to worship in the mosque. But to emphasize, in the interest of promoting inter faith collegiality, such elements of hospitality in the narrative over against the essential thrust of the narrative is entirely to misread the verse under discussion. The argument, the language, the tone – every constituent element of the context of *Āl 'Imrān* 3.64 is exclusivist in character. As for the verse's invitation, 'Come now to a word common between us and you', it is not an offer to find middle ground between Christianity and Islam. The Arabic phrase *kalima sawā'* does not mean that the Christian and the Muslim understandings of monotheism are to be added and then divided by two in order to arrive at a mean that would be acceptable to both parties. Simply put, the phrase urges the claims of the Muslim interpretation of monotheism over against those of the Christian interpretation.

The third verse I wish to examine is this:

> Say: 'People of the Book, you do not stand on anything, until you perform the Torah and the Gospel, and what was sent down to you from your Lord.'[17]

This verse is seen as sanctioning Judaism and Christianity in almost absolute terms and, consequently, as implying that Islam can hold a dialogue with the two religions in whatever form they might exist. Again, this interpretation completely misses the thrust of the verse. The verse does not aim simply to remind Jews and Christians to remain true to their own scriptures and to assure them that, if they follow their own scriptures, then they do not need the Qur'ān. Read in its context, the verse is clearly polemical in character. It argues that Jews and Christians are *not* following their scriptures, a point made only two verses earlier with the words, 'Had they performed the Torah and the Gospel . . .' (*wa-law annahum aqāmu t-Tawrāta wa-l-Injīla . . .*).[18]

I have tried to show that the Muslim use of some of the Qur'ānic verses to argue for the desirability of inter faith dialogue is suspect. So far I have not said anything about my own view of inter faith dialogue. Before I do so, however, I would allow myself a digression about the rationale of such dialogue.

The credit for initiating and sustaining inter faith dialogue goes largely to Christians. Major Christian organizations as well as prominent Christians – the Archbishop of Canterbury among them – have invested time, effort and resources in promoting such dialogue. With a few exceptions, the Muslim participation in the dialogue in terms of range, commitment and sophistication has been, perhaps, largely reactive. Be that as it may, inter faith dialogue is, essentially, a Western phenomenon; unless I am much mistaken, very little of such dialogue takes place in the East. In several Asian and African countries, Muslim and Christian missionaries go about seeking converts. They are supported in this endeavour by resourceful organizations based in other countries, and their missionary activities are seldom hampered by inter faith qualms. What, then, is the rationale for inter faith dialogue in the West? One of the reasons given by several Christian writers is that faith-based dialogue is needed to stem the tide of secularism and to further the cause of a God-oriented ethics. This argument needs to be examined critically. First, an inter faith dialogue aimed at strengthening the bonds between religious communities with the overt aim of countering the forces of secularism would appear to be only redrawing the battle-lines because it replaces one fault-line – that represented by conflict between religions – by another – that represented by conflict between religion and secularism. But this is no more than a realignment of the fighting forces, and one might ask whether this realignment would truly serve the larger cause of inter faith dialogue – namely, the cause of promoting peace and harmony in the world? Secondly, an interreligious alliance made in the face of a secularist threat can only be tactical in nature; it is likely to lose its rationale if the threat ceases to exist, thus allowing the faiths to lapse into conflict. In some regions of the world, ethnic or tribal rivalries are suspended in the face of a foreign invasion but resurface when the invasion is vacated. An inter faith understanding along similar lines is likely to suffer a similar fate.

It is time for you to ask me: If this is what you think of inter faith dialogue, then how do you account for your presence at this seminar? My response to the question is twofold. First, what I have said is part of what I think about inter faith dialogue; it is not all of what I think about it. I have said that some of the Qur'ān-based arguments offered in justification of inter faith dialogue are questionable. The statement only underscores the need to probe deeper for answers. My contention is that the Qur'ān – or any other scripture – cannot be mined for just about any answers to just about any questions. It is not right to take scripture for granted. It is not right to think of scripture as a hat that would yield rabbits of desired colours and sizes. It is not right to do violence to the context of scripture in order to wrench out of it supposedly politically correct responses. This brings me to my second point.

In my view, the failure to ground inter faith dialogue credibly in the Qur'ān is due primarily to a failure to develop a Qur'ān-based theology of inter faith dialogue. Instead of fumbling for odd or isolated Qur'ānic verses on which to base the case for such dialogue, we need to look at the Qur'ān as a whole, perhaps Archimedes-like standing 'outside' the Qur'ān in order to take an integral view of it and then to elicit, in light of its overall ethos, its response to our questions.

The Qur'ānic event was accompanied by the Prophetic event. On Muslim belief, the Qur'ān was given to and proclaimed by Muhammad, a prophet of God. Now a prophet, by definition, speaks in categorical terms. A prophet does not invite people to tea parties at which to hold academic discussions with them on issues of common interest. Decisiveness is one of the hallmarks of a prophet's speech. Isaiah does not say, 'You have a slight headache.' He says:

> The whole head is sick, and the whole heart faint.
> From the sole of the foot even to the head, there is no soundness in it,
> but bruises and sores and bleeding wounds;
> they have not been drained, or bound up, or softened with oil.[19]

When the Lord puts his hand out and touches Jeremiah's mouth, he does not say to him, 'I confer on you the status of an observer at the United Nations.' He says:

> Now, I have put my words in your mouth.
> See, today I appoint you over nations and over kingdoms,
> to pluck up and to pull down,
> to destroy and to overthrow,
> to build and to plant.[20]

The same Jesus who says, 'Go and learn what this means, "I desire mercy, not sacrifice" ',[21] also says:

> Do not think that I have come to bring peace to the earth; I have not come to bring peace, but a sword.
>
> For I have come to set a man against his father,
> and a daughter against her mother,
> and a daughter-in-law against her mother-in-law;
> and one's foes will be members of one's household.[22]

There is nothing strange about this biblical profile of the prophet – a profile that Muhammad fits – as long as we remember that prophecy is serious business and a prophet means business. Being God's direct appointee and serving as his mouthpiece, the prophet speaks in decisive, black-and-white terms precisely because he is possessed of a special authority.[23] Ordinary believers, on the other hand, cannot speak in decisive, black-and-white terms simply because they are not prophets and do not have a prophet's authority; they can neither call down the curse of plague on the House of Pharaoh nor cleave the waters for the people of Israel. This does not mean that ordinary believers cannot have a strong faith commitment; it only means that they cannot act on behalf of God, as would a prophet. The post-prophetic period, it seems to me, is in some sense qualitatively different from the prophetic period, and it is in the distinction between the two periods that the clues to an authentic theology of inter faith dialogue may be found and developed. What we need, then, is a post-prophetic theology of inter faith dialogue. I am intuitively convinced that such a theology is possible, and that explains my presence here. But, frankly, I do not know what the details of the substance and structure of that theology might be. There are, however, a few important clues I find in the Qur'ān, and I would like to conclude by discussing them briefly.

Quite apart from the Qur'ān's dire warnings to those who reject its message is the Qur'ān's explicit approval of the quality of sincerity of faith and commitment. The Qur'ān states that Abraham 'came to his Lord with a wholesome heart' (*idh jā'a Rabbahū bi-qalbin salīmin*),[24] and that, on the Day of Judgement, salvation will belong to 'those who possess a wholesome heart' (*illā man ata llāha bi-qalbin salīmin*).[25] Reading the Qur'ānic dictum about the wholesome heart in light of the distinction drawn above between the prophetic and the post-prophetic periods, one can say that a prophet, who receives direct guidance from God, may very well know who possesses a wholesome heart and who does not and may, therefore, be in a position to judge the quality of faith of this or that individual, but that this privileged position is denied to others. The imperative to refrain from passing such judgement generates another imperative – that of treating others' beliefs with respect, tolerance and understanding.

The Qur'ān's emphasis on the wholesomeness of the heart ties in with its emphasis on individual accountability. With reference to the Day of Judgement, God will say to human beings: 'Now you have come to Us one by one, as We created you upon the first time.'[26] The notion of individual accountability signifies that, in the final analysis, it is the worth of the individual as an individual that matters. Here, I believe, is room for developing what I have called a post-prophetic theology of inter faith dialogue.

Hospitable readings: Comments on *Scriptures in Dialogue*

Miroslav Volf

I am honoured and delighted that the organizers have invited me to participate in this year's 'Building Bridges' seminar. But they have given me an unenviable task. I show up as the new kid on the block, and immediately I have to offer reflections on the previous year's seminar. Many of you were at that seminar and are equipped with all the knowledge of insiders. The only thing I have before me is the record of the seminar, entitled *Scriptures in Dialogue*[27] – and, I should add, an enthusiastic personal report from a participant who, unfortunately, is not here this year, Professor David Ford. I comfort myself, though, with the thought that an outsider can occasionally see things from a fresh vantage point, both confirming and challenging the self-perceptions of insiders.

As I understand it, my task is not to offer a comprehensive evaluation of the previous 'Building Bridges' seminar but, much more modestly, to give you my take on it. Hence I will offer you a series of loosely related comments dealing with (1) the importance of the seminar, (2) its key methodological decisions, and (3) its main feature, namely the practice of Christians and Muslims reading their scriptures together. I will conclude with two comments of a more personal nature.

Importance

I will be brief on the importance of Muslim–Christian dialogue. The participants in the Qatar seminar must have had a sense of immense weight of their endeavour – weight, in the sense in which the term is used by Milan Kundera in his book *The Unbearable Lightness of Being* and by Friedrich Nietzsche, from whom Kundera borrowed it. The war of the coalition forces led by the USA against Iraq had barely begun. In the minds of many people on the street – likely even in the minds of some of those sitting in war rooms – it was a war between Christians and Muslims, even if it was not a war in which religion was the primary motivation. The Iraq war was, of course, not the only recent war in which Christians and Muslims stood on opposite sides of the firing lines. In the region from which I come, Southeast Europe, battles were raging between Christians and Muslims less than a decade ago. Even as I write these lines, violent clashes are taking place in Kosovo, leaving in their trail scores of dead and injured as well as a number of Orthodox and Muslim houses of worship burned to the ground, including a seventeenth-century mosque in Belgrade. In a context marked by violence, engagements that foster deeper mutual understanding between Christians and Muslims are signs and enactments – symbols! – of an alternative future, even if they have little immediate impact upon warring parties.

The seminar's *present-day political* importance pales in comparison with its *long-term global* importance. A quick look at statistics will, I hope, suffice to make my point obvious. There are more than two billion Christians and more than one billion Muslims in the world today. Even more significant than these staggering numbers – more than one-half of the world's population belongs to one of our two religious communities! – are projections about the growth of these communities in the future. Christianity and Islam are close competitors in the race to be the fastest-growing religion in the world today, with other religions as well as secularism lagging significantly behind. (By now we all know that secularism is not the future of our world, as some very influential Western thinkers have believed over the past two centuries, but a mistaken vision of that future.)

Relations between these two largest and fastest-growing religious traditions are presently marked by tension and sometimes even hostility and war. Whether our global future will be bleak or bright depends greatly on the quality of the relationship between Christians and Muslims. Other powerful forces are shaping our world as well, such as the markets, globalization, and the breathtaking speed of technological advances. But religion is clearly a force to be reckoned with, and the most powerful religions in the foreseeable future – most numerous and most culturally and politically significant – will be Christianity and Islam.

Methodological decisions

1. After reading *Scriptures in Dialogue,* I concluded that in Qatar there was virtually *no reflection on method.* How refreshing! I have come to believe that the obsession with method is a bane of modern Christian theology. We spend so much time thinking about how to do theology that we end up hardly ever *doing* any of it! Jeffery Stout has compared methodological reflection with throat-clearing and added that if you just keep clearing your throat, it won't be long before you will lose your audience.

Obsession with method has come to be a bane of inter faith engagements as well. Too many inter faith dialogues are mainly about how to conduct a dialogue – what its presuppositions, its procedures, and its aims should be. Not so in Qatar. Instead of spending most of their time clearing throats, the participants dared actually to speak and did so with conviction and eloquence. No doubt, a great deal of methodological reflection preceded the seminar, and a great deal will follow it. A fine piece of such subsequent methodological reflection is Archbishop Rowan Williams's 'Christian theology and other faiths', included in the book but not presented at the seminar. There is no virtue in methodological ignorance, of course. We rightly want method to be appropriate to our subject, and so we reflect on method and keep refining it as we go along. Presumably that is why I was asked to comment on the previous seminar at the beginning of this one. But methodological reflection cannot be the show itself. It must happen off-stage and draw its purpose and subject matter from what is occurring on-stage. 'The show must go on', said the participants of the Qatar seminar to themselves – and they dared to begin in the middle.

2. The absence of explicit methodological reflection notwithstanding, the seminar shows a great deal of *methodological sophistication.* Interreligious dialogues are often conducted in one of two ways. The discussions centre either on specifically religious convictions – distinctive beliefs of respective communities – or on the activities in the world these communities deem important. Proponents of these two approaches to inter faith dialogue – we can call the two approaches doctrinal and ethical – often engage in sharp disputes. As a Christian theologian, I think of the rifts within the World Council of Churches between 'Faith and Order' folks and 'Life and Work' folks! What the quarrelling advocates of 'doctrine dialogues' or of 'ethics dialogues' often fail to note is how much they have in common. They both presuppose a relatively sharp division between specifically religious thought and generically human practices and therefore also a rift between religious and non-religious spheres. Such separation is by no means a given, however; it is an intellectual and practical construct of modernity. Gotthold Lessing pressed for such separation in *Nathan the Wise* by calling his readers first to be human and then Jews, Christians, or Muslims; Immanuel Kant argued for it in *Religion within the Boundaries of Mere Reason* by claiming that whereas morality is single and universal, faiths are plural and particular and should therefore be subservient to morality.

Both Christian and Muslim traditions contest in their own ways such separation between religious and generically human spheres. As Archbishop Williams has pointed out in his essay for the book, 'religions' are 'a variety of styles of living, each of which has a very different account of the world as a whole, life as a whole'. Consequently, 'disagreements between religious traditions are very significantly disagreements about the kind of universe we inhabit, what that universe makes possible for human beings; and what is the most truthful or adequate or even sane way of behaving in the universe'.[28] If he is right – and I think he is – then the dialogue between religious traditions must always be about comprehensive ways of life that include thought and action and not about 'beliefs' or 'activities'. The strength of the Qatar seminar was that its procedures were in harmony with what faiths are – comprehensive ways of life, not just beliefs about the world above or rules for actions in the world below.

3. Christianity and Islam are ways of life lived in reference to God. In religious reflection – in theology – we think therefore about everything *sub ratione dei*, or under the aspect of its relation to God. It follows that in inter faith dialogues, 'God' cannot be primarily one among many discrete themes – a theme we can take up or maybe leave untouched for a while in order to devote ourselves to more pressing needs. Rather, 'God' must be the reference point in regard to which all themes are discussed. Of course, 'God' can be taken up as a special theme – as when Muslims and Christians debate the nature of God's oneness – for God is something quite apart from the world. But the world would be nothing apart from God, and so when Christians and Muslims speak about their ways of life, no theme can be taken up without relating it to God.

I was struck with how prominent a place God occupied in the Qatar seminar, in contrast with many other dialogues in which I have participated or about which I have read. God was not thematized as an otherworldly reality unrelated to everyday life but as the pivot of Muslim and Christian ways of life. And this, I think, is exactly as it ought to be. Our sacred traditions have always insisted that human beings must be oriented toward God because they and their world were created by God. Approaches that bracket the question of God miss what Islam and Christianity are all about and instead enact a modernist reading of religions as nothing but human ways of strengthening, comforting, and orienting ourselves in the world.

Scriptures in dialogue

The two features of the Qatar seminar that I have just highlighted – the treatment of faiths as ways of life and the centrality of God – are, I believe, consequences of a very simple but momentous decision to organize the seminar around reading the sacred scriptures together. For the scriptures themselves are the Word of God addressed to people, to the people of God in the midst of their daily lives. In addition to pushing conference participants to reflect on faith as a way of life before God, there are other important advantages of reading the Bible and the Qur'ān together.

1. The first concerns the way in which reading the scriptures together brings *movement* to *calcified positions* – an advantage that may not be apparent at first glance. We might fear that appealing to the scriptures could close off further discussion. After all, a community's scriptures are its final authority. By appealing to them, interlocutors could easily come to the point where they would say to each other, 'Our scripture says this and your scripture says that, and that's that!' and be off to the next subject or, more distressingly, go their separate ways. It may be better, the argument could continue, to discuss our communally significant convictions and practices.

And yet exactly the opposite may be the case. Take the scriptures away, and we have little to say when, after prolonged and strenuous disagreement, our interlocutors tell us, 'This is what we think; this is what we do' – except to do a very unhelpful thing of accusing them of being either irrational or irresponsible. Put the scriptures at the centre of the dialogue, and the deadlock can be avoided. The disputes are now less about us and our opinions and more about something that has a claim on us and to which we give greater allegiance than we do to our own convictions. I very much like the title of the Qatar seminar – *Scriptures in Dialogue*. In an important sense, *we are not so much agents of a dialogue as instruments of a dialogue whose main protagonists are our respective scriptures*. Put differently, the dialogue is not primarily about us; or rather, it is about us only because it is about the scriptures. As long as we hold onto the scriptures, we can loosen the grip with which we hold onto our own convictions. We are firmly rooted and yet open to change.

For introducing movement to calcified positions, almost as important as the authority of the scriptures is their *immense richness*. They are like the surface of the ocean I see from my office window, always the same and yet always changing, depending on light, wind, and the tides. Or, if one prefers a more solid metaphor, they are like a beautiful mountain peak, solid and immovable and yet always changing as the seasons change, as the sun falls on it from different angles as we circle around it. The richness of the scriptures – 'inexhaustibility' is probably the right word – is a further reason why the dialogue around them can be so fruitful. Given both the authority and complexity of scripture, a rich and continuing discussion can ensue with the potential to change both parties without threatening their identities as people of this or that Holy Book.

2. The 'Scriptures in Dialogue' approach offers resources for dealing with the question of *identity and otherness*. In inter faith relations, there is a tendency either to be fascinated with commonalities and relegate differences to insignificance or to be obsessed with differences and disregard commonalities. In the first case specific identities are compromised, and in the second they are enacted in an oppositional way. The importance of using the 'Scriptures in Dialogue' approach for the first problem is obvious: the scriptures are the authoritative word whose content gives a community's religious identity its contours. Let me briefly address the importance of the method only for the second problem – oppositional construction of identity.

Identity is construed oppositionally when I define myself as what the other is not, when I see my identity as pure, freed from the presence of the other. If communal convictions figure prominently in inter faith dialogues, it is easy to bracket commonalities and concentrate on differences. After all, religious convictions form a more or less integrated whole, and because the wholes differ, even those convictions that two groups may share can in fact be different. Hence we may be justified in concluding that we are simply 'us', and we are 'us' precisely in that we differ from 'them'.

But the conclusion is mistaken. Even among different systems, there can be significant overlaps. Concentrate on the scriptures rather than on beliefs, and the mistake is less likely to happen – or at least, it is less likely to happen in dialogue between Jews, Christians and Muslims. For these three communities have significant portions of their scriptures in common. This holds true even though there are differences between the Bible and Qur'ān as to the exact content of Torah (*Tawrāt*), Psalms (*Zabūr*) and Gospel (*Injīl*). As a consequence, among these three communities the other is always part of the self, and their identities cannot be understood in simple opposition. Take St John's Gospel, for example. It is the New Testament text that contains the strongest negative statements about 'the Jews'. And yet it does not construe Christian identity as 'non-Jewish' – it claims that salvation is from the Jews – because it considers Jewish scripture to be also Christian scripture. From a Christian perspective, to hold Christian convictions is not simply to hold non-Jewish convictions but to integrate Jewish convictions into one's own. The same holds true, in a somewhat different way, in regard to Islam.

3. The final advantage of the 'Scriptures in Dialogue' method is related to the fact that in the past Christians and Muslims have made war against each other using the scriptures. We often engaged in interpretative endeavours as self-enclosed entities; we interpreted scripture not just to bolster our own identity in the face of the other but also to put down the other, even to harm the other.

As a Christian, I consider such interpretations of scripture sinful, even when they are formally correct. At the heart of the Christian faith lies a claim that, out of incomprehensible love, our Lord Jesus Christ died for us while we were still God's enemies and therefore, as those who are called to imitate Christ, we can and must love all people, even our enemies. When we interpret other communities, whether of friends or enemies, such love demands that we try to see them as they see themselves and to see ourselves as they see us. When we interpret the scriptures, such love demands that we enter sympathetically into others' efforts to interpret their scriptures as well as listen to how they perceive us as readers of our own scriptures.[29] In other words, we are called to practise interpretive hospitality – visiting each other's interpretive homes and exchanging gifts as we do so. Such hospitality will not necessarily lead to agreement in the interpretation of our respective scriptures. And it will certainly not lead to agreement between our communities for the simple reason that we hold very distinct – even if overlapping – texts as authoritative. But such interpretive hospitality will help us not only better understand our own and others' scriptures but also disincline us from interpreting them in opposition to each other.

To practise such hospitable readings of each other's scriptures, we do not have to consider them as somehow on the same footing, on a par as God's revelation. We may well consider different scriptures as a revisable prophetic Word of God or indeed as nothing more than powerful and influential human word. Yet even with such stances – stances which the majority of Christians and Muslims espouse – it is possible and fruitful to practise hospitable readings of each other's Holy Book(s).

Concluding observations

In conclusion, two comments of a more personal nature.

The first, under the title *presence and abstraction*, concerns my own experience of reading *Scriptures in Dialogue*. As a Christian, I was moved by texts from the Qur'ān and by Muslim interpretations of them. I was left cold, however, by the accompanying reflections – a discrete section of the book – in which Christian and Muslim texts and interpretations were compared and contrasted. For me, the first was a full-blooded presence, alive and uncontrollable; the second was a somewhat bloodless abstraction, inert and manageable. Not that I found the reflections useless. To the contrary, I learned a great deal from them about differences and similarities between Christianity and Islam. But the texts from the Qur'ān and their Muslim interpretations opened new worlds to me and let me see the Bible with new eyes. While theological reflections were informative, the readings of sacred texts were generative.

I am not sure that this observation has any import for how we should conduct the present dialogue. For my experience may be little more than an echo of my own propensity for constructive engagement with religious traditions rather than for their comparative analysis. My sense is, though, that the 'Scriptures in Dialogue' project is at heart a constructive one – a project in which engaged interpreters of scripture speak to other engaged interpreters of scripture and to communities that are shaped by scripture. If so, then comparative reflections will not be the culmination of our engagements, not even a provisional one, but always a transitional midpoint from which to return to the sacred texts.

My last comment has to do with the *power and vulnerability* of the scriptures. I was struck with participants' sense of scripture's power. Scripture is the world we inhabit; it is the fountain that cannot be drunk dry; its presence in the soul is life giving, and hence we seek to learn it by heart and to let it structure our life rhythms. Scripture has power, Christians and Muslims believe, because it is God's Word. And as the Prophet says, God's Word will not return empty without accomplishing that for which it has been sent.

And yet, its power notwithstanding, scripture is at the same time 'immensely vulnerable', as Tim Winter has written. 'It is probably fair', he explains, 'to observe that nowhere has human ingenuity been more destructively abused than in the realm of scriptural interpretation.'[30] It is not clear that either Christian or Muslim tradition has the means to ward off interpretative abuses, except by trusting in

God's grace and by inculcating the need for holiness and spiritual attentiveness on the part of the readers.

A diffuse but important tradition in Christianity insists that saints are the best interpreters of the scriptures. They have the eyes to see and ears to hear, and it is on account of their saintliness that scripture is 'hagiologically fertile'. No doubt, it is the Word of God that made these people into saints; the saints did not make the communities' sacred texts into the Word of God. Yet to function as holy, scripture is dependent on holy readers. In the hands of the corrupt – in the hands of those who are greedy for power, riches and glory – the scriptures will be fertile in spawning evil deeds, as history shows. Powerful as scripture is, it is also vulnerable, caught in the struggle between the holiness and the baseness of its readers. As we participate in this seminar, may we be readers worthy of great treasures contained in our Holy Book(s)!

2

Called by God

This chapter comprises studies of four scriptural passages, two dialogues each pairing texts from the Bible and from the Qur'ān. All describe, in different ways, the experience of a human being encountering the divine, and being commissioned by God as a chosen agent of the divine Word. In the case of the biblical passages, one describes the calling of a prophet, the other the calling of an apostle; in the case of the Qur'ān, such a distinction cannot be maintained in the category of divinely appointed messengers. For Muslims and Christians alike, authentic prophetic or apostolic activity can only begin at this point, in encounter with the transcendent God who is the source and goal of all being.

Scripture dialogue I

Ṭā Hā 20.1-36; Exodus 3.1-14

The two passages discussed here show some striking similarities in the ways in which they describe the calling of the prophet Moses. There are several clear points of agreement in the two narratives: for example, God speaks to Moses out of a fire; he tells him to remove his shoes in recognition of the holiness of the place; he directs him to go to Pharaoh to speak.[1] Underlying these obvious parallels, there is the deeper correspondence of the choice and commissioning by God of a human prophet to bear his message to the world. However, it is also important to recognize the different contexts within which these two narratives are set, the different emphases of their messages, and the different purposes they serve.

Ṭā Hā 20.1-36

This Qur'ānic passage is the opening of one of several long presentations of the prophetic figure of Moses (*Mūsā*). After a further sixty-two verses, the treatment of Moses will conclude with the words: 'We relate to you [Prophet] stories of what happened before.'[2] In the same way, this narrative is introduced by God as a retrieval of prophetic history designed to comfort Muhammad in his contemporary delivery of the divine message. The purposes for which the past is recovered are exemplary and edificatory: to demonstrate the recurring patterns of obstinacy and rebellion which God's messengers have always encountered, and to strengthen them and their followers in their obedience. The ability of these verses to deliver that function would be enhanced if it could be assumed that Muhammad's Makkan auditors already had some knowledge of the story of Moses.

Qur'ānic text

[1]*Ṭā Hā*

[2]It was not to distress you [Prophet] that We sent down the Qur'ān to you, [3]but as a reminder for those who hold God in awe, [4]a revelation from the One who created the earth and the high heaven, [5]the Lord of Mercy, established on the throne. [6]Everything in the heavens and on earth, everything between them, everything beneath the soil, belongs to Him. [7]Whatever you may say aloud, He knows what you keep secret and what is even more hidden. [8]God – there is no god but Him – the most excellent names belong to Him.

[9]Has the story of Moses come to you [Prophet]? [10]He saw a fire and said to his people, 'Stay here – I can see a fire. Maybe I can bring you a flaming brand from it or find some guidance there.' [11]When he came to the fire, he was summoned, 'Moses! [12]I am your Lord. Take off your shoes: you are in the sacred valley of Tuwa. [13]I have chosen you, so listen to what is being revealed. [14]I am God; there is no god but Me. So worship Me and keep up the prayer so that you remember Me. [15]The Hour is coming – though I choose to keep it hidden – for each soul to be rewarded for its labour. [16]Do not let anyone who does not believe in it and follows his own desires distract you from it, and so bring you to ruin.

[17]'Moses, what is that in your right hand?' [18]'It is my staff,' he said, 'I lean on it; restrain my sheep with it; I also have other uses for it.' [19]God said, 'Throw it down, Moses.' [20]He threw it down and – lo and behold! – it became a fast-moving snake! [21]He said, 'Pick it up without fear: We shall turn it back to its former state. [22]Now place your hand under your armpit: it will come out white, though unharmed: that is another sign. [23]We do this to show you some of Our greatest signs. [24]Go to Pharaoh, for he has truly become a tyrant.' [25]Moses said, 'Lord, lift up my heart [26]and ease my task for me. [27]Untie my tongue [28]so that they may understand my words [29]and give me a helper from my family, [30]my brother Aaron – [31]augment my strength through him. [32]Let him share my task [33]so that we can

glorify You much 34and remember You often: 35You are always watching over us.'
36God said, 'Moses, your request is granted.'

Commentary

The Qur'ānic account of Moses' call, embedded as an exemplary illustration within God's address to the prophet Muhammad, is almost devoid of elements tying it to a particular historical context. The message entrusted to Moses is that of absolute monotheism, the necessity of prayer and the coming judgement (14-15). This is set in a theological framework which emphasizes divine mercy, transcendence and omniscience (5-7). The direction to Moses to visit Pharaoh (24) is given only after the enunciation of this eternal and universal truth, and Moses according to this passage neither explicitly accepts this mission nor seeks to negotiate with God about its terms.[3] The figure of the prophet thus functions as an immediately available instrument of the divine purpose.

In Moses' case, God endorses the validity of the prophetic message by accompanying it with 'signs' (17-23). It is Islamic belief that the authenticity of the prophets' messages can be confirmed by the miracles (*mu'jizāt*) which accompany them.[4] Demands for a sign had arisen in the reception of Muhammad's own preaching, but the primary sign given in that case[5] was the inimitably miraculous character (*i'jāz*)[6] of the Qur'ānic text itself; in a sense, the type of external *mu'jiza* here associated with Moses was superseded.

When Moses goes on to make the request of God that he should be accompanied by his brother Aaron (29-34), he does so not to seek to excuse himself but because this will allow for a more efficacious delivery of the message. In Islamic thought, 'prophetology' (*nubuwwat*) has become a highly developed area of theological thought, with clear criteria established for the recognition of those who are charged with an authentic prophetic mission – criteria which would exclude the presence of a speech defect.[7] *Nubuwwat* teaches a high view of the prophets' status: while no more than human beings, their sinless status would preclude any refusal to obey the divine order. *Nubuwwat* also effectively assimilates all prophetic experience into one pattern, which is then most fully exemplified in Muhammad. The Qur'ānic passages concerning pre-Muhammadan prophets, therefore, on the one hand show that these figures do indeed satisfy the criteria of *nubuwwat*, and acceptance of their messages is a part of Islamic belief. On the other hand the Qur'ān also implies that their separate witness is no longer required in the post-Muhammadan situation, marked as it is by the revelation of the final message through the final messenger, whose virtues reproduce and excel all of his predecessors'.

1. Twenty-nine of the sūras of the Qur'ān begin in this way with a letter or sequence of letters. The significance of these opening verses has been much debated by Muslims. Some have sought to discern a hidden meaning or a mystic symbolism in them; others have seen them as being among those verses the meaning of which is accessible only to God.[8] With regard to the specific letters *Ṭā Hā*, which occur only at the beginning of this sūra, one traditional interpretation[9] reads them as a dialect form of the vocative meaning 'O man!' This would imply a universal audience for this message (in which case the person addressed in verse 2 would be not the Prophet but any human who is a reader or hearer of the Qur'ān).

5. The phrase 'established (*istawā*) on the throne', which occurs at other points in the Qur'ān also, has been a focus of exegetical controversy in Islamic theology, because of its apparently anthropomorphic way of referring to God. It can metaphorically be interpreted as a reference to God's supreme authority.

8. The compact theology of this verse co-ordinates two principles. The first is the opening part of the core Islamic witness (*shahāda*) to the sole existence of the divine being – a statement which will be repeated by God himself in verse 14. Following this is one of several Qur'ānic references to the multiplicity of names through which this God can be known in his attributes. Islamic tradition counted these as ninety-nine in number, with a hundredth name (according to some, unknown, according to others, the name Allah) pointing to his unknowable essence.[10]

11-13. Muslim theologians extensively discussed the sense in which Moses could have 'heard' the divine voice. The point at issue here was whether this was the uncreated Word of God, or a sound created by God in the fire to convey his message.

12. In the Qur'ān, Moses' encounter with God is in a valley, not on the mountain as in Exodus. *Tuwa* is probably a proper place-name, though some interpret it as 'twice-blessed'.

14. God repeats in first person form the *shahāda* which has already been expressed in the third person in verse 8.

23. The Qur'ānic 'sign' (*āya*) can be any demonstration of God's power – here, miraculous signs, but elsewhere also the natural phenomena of creation, or the text of scripture itself (an individual verse is an *āya*).[11]

29. The word here translated 'helper' is *wazīr*, used in later Muslim political contexts to denote a 'minister' assisting a ruler. A tradition of the Prophet often cited by Shi'ites associates Moses' request to God for a *wazīr* from his own family with Muhammad's later designation of his son-in-law Ali as his successor: 'Muhammad said to Ali: "Are you not content to be with respect to me as Aaron was to Moses, except that after me there shall be no other prophet".'[12] In Sufi exegesis, Aaron (*Hārūn*) became the symbol of esotericism in distinction to the exoteric Moses (*Mūsā*).

Exodus 3.1-14

In its biblical context, Moses' encounter with God is dramatically poised between a description of the sufferings of the Israelites and the epic story of their liberation through the exodus. Rather than retrieving lessons from the past to apply to the present, this passage presents the theophany as a pivotal chapter in the divine history which continually identifies and moulds one nation to live as the people of God. The calling of Moses as a biblical prophet implies a relationship with that people, and leads to at least a partial revelation of the God who will bind himself in a covenant with them. Instead of prefacing the story of Moses with a theological statement, the Exodus story has the divine name emerge at the end of a conversation between God and his prophet.

Biblical text

[1]Moses was keeping the flock of his father-in-law Jethro, the
priest of Midian; he led his flock beyond the wilderness, and
came to Horeb, the mountain of God. [2]There the angel of the
Lord appeared to him in a flame of fire out of a bush; he looked,
and the bush was blazing, yet it was not consumed. [3]Then Moses
said, 'I must turn aside and look at this great sight, and see why
the bush is not burned up.' [4]When the Lord saw that he had
turned aside to see, God called to him out of the bush, 'Moses,
Moses!' And he said, 'Here I am.' [5]Then he said, 'Come no closer!
Remove the sandals from your feet, for the place on which you
are standing is holy ground.' [6]He said further, 'I am the God of
your father, the God of Abraham, the God of Isaac, and the God
of Jacob.' And Moses hid his face, for he was afraid to look at God.
[7]Then the Lord said, 'I have observed the misery of my people
who are in Egypt; I have heard their cry on account of their
taskmasters. Indeed, I know their sufferings, [8]and I have come
down to deliver them from the Egyptians, and to bring them up
out of that land to a good and broad land, a land flowing with
milk and honey, to the country of the Canaanites, the Hittites,
the Amorites, the Perizzites, the Hivites, and the Jebusites. [9]The
cry of the Israelites has now come to me; I have also seen how
the Egyptians oppress them. [10]So come, I will send you to Pharaoh to bring my people, the Israelites, out of Egypt.' [11]But Moses
said to God, 'Who am I that I should go to Pharaoh, and bring
the Israelites out of Egypt?' [12]He said, 'I will be with you; and this
shall be the sign for you that it is I who sent you: when you have

> brought the people out of Egypt, you shall worship God on this mountain.'
> [13]But Moses said to God, 'If I come to the Israelites and say to them, "The God of your ancestors has sent me to you," and they ask me, "What is his name?" what shall I say to them?' [14]God said to Moses, 'I AM WHO I AM'. He said further, 'Thus you shall say to the Israelites, "I AM has sent me to you." '

Commentary

The biblical narrative is bound up with the specificity of one person and one people. The divine presence on the mountain is occasioned by, and wholly oriented towards, the presence of Moses, and there is discernible a certain reciprocity of presence and action between God and his prophet (4,7). The divine intervention which issues from this theophany is motivated by sympathy for the sufferings of Israel, and designed to lead to that people's liberation (7-8). God here is manifestly partisan, his purposes set against those cast in this drama as the enemies of Israel – not only, immediately, the Egyptians, but also, prospectively, the current inhabitants of Canaan (8).

This sense of partiality is amplified by the elusive hints given here as to the divine identity. The interpretation of the 'I am' formula (14) is disputed. It may indeed be intended in part to prevent any improper sense of 'ownership' of God by Israel. However, there is conversely no doubt that God is the owner of Israel, and his special commitment to them is guaranteed by his own association of his identity with that of the Israelite patriarchs Abraham, Isaac and Jacob (6). This assertion of the rootedness of God's history in the genealogy of a particular people provided a challenge for Christianity as it came to understand itself as a universal faith; in contemporary Christian theology there remain several different ways of understanding the current place of God's covenant promises to Israel.[13] At an immediately existential level, in so far as the story of exodus has echoed powerfully as a symbol of the divinely willed liberation of the oppressed, people of many races have understood themselves to be in the place of those whom Moses leads out to freedom.[14]

The divine relationship with the people of Israel renewed through Moses has a dimension of partnership to it. God will himself travel down to Egypt with his prophet (8,12). There is no expectation that theirs will be a problem-free journey. Moses himself recognizes that his own people's likely initial response will be one of disbelief (13) – as indeed proves to be the case. There will be a strong sense in the Exodus narrative of Moses being caught in the middle between Israel and Israel's God. Yet, paradoxically, this very sense of isolation from his own people increases the prophet's sense of intimacy with the Lord, and this passage sees the first of several episodes in which one of the prophetic roles is to intercede in a way which comes very close to bargaining with God.

2. The sign of the unconsumed burning bush has been a rich source of symbolism for both Jews and Christians. Philo sees it as representing the oppressed people of Israel, who 'would not be destroyed by those who were attacking them'.[15] In patristic exegesis, it came to be seen as a typological figure pointing to Mary, who bore God without either being consumed or losing her virginity.[16]

4. The repetition of a person's name is characteristic of divine call narratives in the Hebrew scriptures. Note that Moses' response, 'Here I am (*hinnēnī*)', underlines the importance of the presence of this particular human individual as a counterpart to the presence of God.[17]

This verse brings together the two ways in which the divine is referred to in the narrative before he himself responds to Moses' question about his name: firstly, 'the Lord' (*yhwh* – also in verses 2,7); and secondly, 'God' (*elōhīm* – also in verses 6 [in construct with the patriarchs], 11-14).

6. Unlike the Qur'ānic account, this verse implies the possibility of a vision of God. In Exodus 33.17ff., it is God himself who protects Moses from the danger of seeing his face. In this passage the directness of a possible vision is somewhat modified by the description of the divine presence as an 'angel' (verse 2).

7. The sequence of actions attributed to God in his attention to his people ('I have observed . . . I have heard . . . I know') exactly mirrors that of Moses in his attention to God in the theophany: he observes the bush, he hears the voice, and he comes to know the name of God. This correspondence between divine and human then prepares the way for Moses' and God's accompaniment of one another on the journey into Egypt (verses 8,12).

10. The Hebrew *lekhah* might be translated as either 'come' or 'go', but the NRSV here follows the Septuagint and the Vulgate in perceptively using an expression which implies a hitherward motion (cf. LXX *deuro*; Vulg. *veni*), since God is inviting Moses to accompany him on a journey he is himself making (verses 8,12).

13. This verse has generated a huge amount of exegesis in Jewish and Christian theology, within which three major strands of interpretation can be distinguished:

(a) The cryptic response may be seen as a deliberate refusal to compromise the divine freedom by making known the name of God.[18]

(b) The Hebrew formula 'I AM [WHO I AM]', *ehyeh* [*asher ehyeh*], may be intended as an etymology of the tetragrammaton *yhwh*, to which it seems close – in which case the latter itself could be expressive of God's dynamism in calling creatures into being.

(c) A more philosophically oriented strand of thought sees this passage as validating the identification of God with 'being itself' – the Septuagint at this point translates 'I AM THE BEING (*ho ōn*)'.[19]

Philo, in a text which seems quite Islamic in its resonances, writes: 'At first say unto them, "I am that I am", that, when they have learned that there is a difference between Him that is and him that is not, they may be further taught that there is no name whatever that can be properly assigned to Me, who am the only being to whom existence belongs.'[20]

Scripture dialogue II

Acts 9.1-22; *al-Muzzammil* 73.1-20

The idea of certain individuals being 'sent' is important for Jews, Christians and Muslims in explaining the ways in which God communicates with humanity. The following two texts present the calling of an 'apostle' in a Christian and in a Muslim setting respectively. While the underlying dynamism of mission in each may be broadly comparable, it is important to be aware of the very different ways in which 'apostleship' is understood in relation to prophethood in either religion. In Islam, the two concepts are roughly interchangeable,[21] but they are distinct in Christianity.[22]

Acts 9.1-22

In Acts 9, the concept of apostolate operates at two different levels. In a general sense, it is the dynamic informing the whole narrative, flowing from the 'sentness' of Jesus and the community with which he is identified, and finding practical realization through members of that community such as Ananias. In a specific and technical sense, it is a vocation and responsibility for which Paul as an individual has been particularly chosen. The dramatic account of his acceptance of this charge serves both to validate his status within the Early Church and also to underline the mark of suffering which will characterize his exercise of the apostolic ministry.

Biblical text

> 1Meanwhile Saul, still breathing threats and murder against the
> disciples of the Lord, went to the high priest 2and asked him for
> letters to the synagogues at Damascus, so that if he found any
> who belonged to the Way, men or women, he might bring them
> bound to Jerusalem. 3Now as he was going along and approach-
> ing Damascus, suddenly a light from heaven flashed around
> him. 4He fell to the ground and heard a voice saying to him,
> 'Saul, Saul, why do you persecute me?' 5He asked, 'Who are you,
> Lord?' The reply came, 'I am Jesus, whom you are persecuting.
> 6But get up and enter the city, and you will be told what you are

to do.' [7]The men who were travelling with him stood speechless because they heard the voice but saw no one. [8]Saul got up from the ground, and though his eyes were open, he could see nothing; so they led him by the hand and brought him into Damascus. [9]For three days he was without sight, and neither ate nor drank.

[10]Now there was a disciple in Damascus named Ananias. The Lord said to him in a vision, 'Ananias.' He answered, 'Here I am, Lord.' [11]The Lord said to him, 'Get up and go to the street called Straight, and at the house of Judas look for a man of Tarsus named Saul. At this moment he is praying, [12]and he has seen in a vision a man named Ananias come in and lay his hands on him so that he might regain his sight. [13]But Ananias answered, 'Lord, I have heard from many about this man, how much evil he has done to your saints in Jerusalem; [14]and here he has authority from the chief priests to bind all who invoke your name.' [15]But the Lord said to him, 'Go, for he is an instrument whom I have chosen to bring my name before Gentiles and kings and before the people of Israel; [16]I myself will show him how much he must suffer for the sake of my name.' [17]So Ananias went and entered the house. He laid his hands on Saul and said, 'Brother Saul, the Lord Jesus, who appeared to you on your way here, has sent me so that you may regain your sight and be filled with the Holy Spirit.' [18]And immediately something like scales fell from his eyes, and his sight was restored. Then he got up and was baptized, [19]and after taking some food, he regained his strength. For several days he was with the disciples in Damascus, [20]and immediately he began to proclaim Jesus in the synagogues, saying, 'He is the Son of God.' [21]All who heard him were amazed and said, 'Is not this the man who made havoc in Jerusalem among those who invoked this name? And has he not come here for the purpose of bringing them bound before the chief priests?' [22]Saul became increasingly more powerful and confounded the Jews who lived in Damascus by proving that Jesus was the Messiah.

Commentary

This famous narrative, often described as the story of Paul's conversion, in fact focuses on his commissioning as an apostle, based on a prior decision by God to call him to this specific task (15). Central to Paul's claim to apostolic status was the experience reported here of seeing the risen Lord Jesus;[23] the text emphasizes that this vision, as distinct from an audition of the heavenly voice, was accessible to Paul only (7). 'Apostolate' for Paul is a form of Christian vocation with distinctive characteristics, and the account here (which presumably can be traced back in its main inflections to his own self-understanding)[24] emphasizes the constitutive role played in it by the experience of suffering. Indeed, Paul is described as the recipient of two successive revelations: the first (5) discloses to him the present sufferings of Jesus in his disciples, and the second (16) announces the suffering he himself will undergo. It is not surprising that the very act of revelation and commissioning should bring Paul into a state of physical brokenness: he falls to the ground and loses his sight (4,8-9).

The text dramatically presents a direct, 'vertical' communication with the risen Jesus in the calling of Paul, and insistence on this is a major emphasis in the apostle's own writings. Yet there is a 'horizontal' dimension too: the role of other Christians, as represented by the disciple Ananias, is indispensable. The passage describes a vision of Jesus to him also, resulting in a parallel commissioning of him for the specific task of reconciling Paul to the Church. This involves him in healing and baptizing Paul (18), and possibly also in administering the Eucharist to him (19).[25] Even Paul's distinctively individual apostolate, then, relies for its inception and validation on others in the community of faith.[26]

The Acts narrative as we have it is set against a theological horizon which both presupposes and proclaims the divine status of the crucified Jesus. Thus, when Paul asks for the name of the figure who has appeared to him, he receives the unambiguous reply: 'I am Jesus' (5);[27] the word 'Lord' throughout refers to the exalted figure of Jesus Christ (5,10f.,17); and Paul's first proclamation in the synagogues is that this man is 'the Son of God'.[28] These are claims which can seem as scandalously mistaken to Muslims today as they did to many of Paul's first Jewish hearers, but it is evident from this passage that they are rooted in Paul's own personal experience of being broken and remade in his encounter with Jesus.

1. Saul was a Hebrew name; the name which the apostle bore as a Roman citizen was the Latin Paul. It is not the case that Saul's name was changed to Paul on his conversion – Acts 13.9, for example, speaks of 'Saul, also known as Paul'. However, as 'Saul' is used in Jewish contexts, and 'Paul' in interaction with Gentiles, the latter naturally was the much more common title in referring to the apostle's Christian ministry.

2. The high priest in Jerusalem exercised authority over diaspora Jewish communities – a pattern which seems to have been carried across into the organization of the earliest Christian communities in the role ascribed to James

(Acts 15.19). His letters constitute Saul as an authorized 'apostle' of temple Judaism – a role which is about to be dramatically reversed.

4. The repetition of the addressee's name is the characteristic formula for a divine call in biblical literature (cf. Exodus 3.4).

5. Following as it does after Saul's commission to attack the Christian community, this verse implies that Jesus himself is persecuted in the persecution of his followers, as a consequence of his mystical solidarity with them.

7. Although the text does not explicitly state that Saul saw Jesus, this is suggested negatively by the insistence that nobody else present did so, and positively in verse 17 by Ananias' words; certainly this was to be Paul's own interpretation of his experience.

9. The 'three days' of insensibility and incapacity may represent a period of death to the old self prior to Saul's being raised up to a new life.

10. 'Lord' here refers specifically to Jesus (cf. verse 14 – 'those who invoke your name').

Ananias' response confirms his attentive presence on God in the *hinnēnī* formula – cf. Exodus 3.4.

15. The sense of having been specially chosen by God for a universal apostolic task is projected backwards by Paul in his own letters to a point before his birth (Galatians 1.15), in this mirroring the pre-birth vocation of Jeremiah to be a 'prophet to the nations' (Jeremiah 1.5).

The image of the apostle as an 'instrument (*skeuos*)' emphasizes his domination by, and subservience to, Christ. It is used by Paul himself (2 Corinthians 4.7, 'treasure in clay vessels') to emphasize the contrast between, on the one hand, the transcendent worth and power of the message of God and, on the other hand, the mortal worthlessness and frailty of the messengers to whom that message is entrusted.

16. This second revelation promised to Saul, by telling of his own suffering, balances that of the suffering of Jesus and the Christians in verse 5.

17. Ananias' laying on of hands is immediately for the recovery of Saul's sight (verse 12), but also points to his commissioning as apostle to the nations (verse 15).

Ananias describes Jesus as having 'appeared' (*ophtheis*) to Saul, using the language of the resurrection narratives and thereby confirming the conferral of apostolic status.

Ananias' status is also that of somebody whom Jesus has 'sent' (*apestalken*) to carry out a specific task: apostolicity is operative within the activities and membership of the entire Christian community, as well as being the special vocation of Paul and others. Jesus in turn is the Holy One sent by the Father as the climax of a prophetic sequence (Acts 7.52); the Lord is both 'apostle' and 'apostoler', the one who is sent and the one who sends.

19. The sequence of laying on of hands followed by baptism has suggested to some that the taking of 'food' (*trophē*) may be a reference to the Eucharist – cf. similarly Acts 16.34.

20,22. Acts describes Paul's activities in two ways – 'proclaiming' (*kērussein*) the divine sonship of Jesus, and 'proving' (*sumbibazein*) his Messiahship. The two are of course closely related, but it is possible to detect a difference in methodology between them: the former has the sense of heraldic announcement, while the latter implies a comparison of evidences for the purpose of argumentative proof. Both form part of the apostolic ministry.

al-Muzzammil 73.1-20

Sūra 73, *al-Muzzammil*, is – with the exception of its final verse, which moves in a rather different context – one of the earliest parts of the Qur'ān to be delivered. It reflects the situation of the early Muslim community in Makka, enthusiastic in its acceptance of revelation but sorely pressed by the hostility of the surrounding pagan society. Within this conflictual environment, Muhammad and his followers are reassured, and their opponents are admonished, by a reminder of the earlier prophetic ministry of Moses. Like Muhammad, Moses was one sent by God (*rasūl*); the persecution the Muslims are now experiencing is shown by this historical example to be an unavoidable part of the prophetic event. There are also suggestions, amplified by subsequent tradition, that suffering is part of the apostolic-prophetic experience in a more personal and interiorized sense also: the very reception of divine revelation is costly for the one chosen as its recipient.

Qur'ānic text

> [1]You [Prophet], enfolded in your cloak! [2]Keep vigil throughout the night, all but a small part of it, [3]half, or a little less, [4]or a little more; recite the Qur'ān slowly and distinctly: [5]We shall send a momentous message down to you. [6]Night prayer makes a deeper impression and sharpens words – [7]you are kept busy for long periods of the day – [8]so celebrate the name of your Lord and devote yourself wholeheartedly to Him. [9]He is Lord of the east and the west, there is no god but Him, so take Him as your Protector, [10]patiently endure what they say, ignore them politely, [11]and leave to Me those who deny the truth and live in comfort. Bear with them for a little while; [12]We have fetters, a blazing fire, [13]food that chokes, and agonizing torment in store for them [14]on the Day when the earth and the mountains will shake. The mountains will become a heap of loose sand.
>
> [15]We have sent a messenger to you [people] to be your witness, just as We sent a messenger to Pharaoh, [16]but Pharaoh disobeyed the messenger and so We inflicted a heavy punishment on him. [17]So if you disbelieve, how can you guard yourselves against a Day that will turn children's hair grey, [18]a Day when the sky will

be torn apart? God's promise will certainly be fulfilled. [19]This is a reminder. Let whoever wishes take the way to his Lord.
[20][Prophet], your Lord is well aware that you sometimes spend nearly two-thirds of the night at prayer – sometimes half, sometimes a third – as do some of your followers. God determines the division of night and day. He knows that you will not be able to keep a measure of it and He has relented towards all of you, so recite as much of the Qur'ān as is easy for you. He knows that some of you will be sick, some of you travelling through the land seeking bounty, some of you fighting in God's way: recite as much as is easy for you, keep up the prayer, pay the prescribed alms, and make God a good loan. Whatever good you store up for yourselves will be improved and increased for you. Ask God for his forgiveness, He is most forgiving, most merciful.

Commentary

The sūra weaves together three interrelated themes: the prophetic experience itself (1,5,8,9); the double reception of the prophetic message, whether acceptance (2-4,6-7) or rejection (10-11); and the differing plans of God in response to this duality, whether for good (20) or for ill (12-19). At the outset, the Prophet is addressed as the 'cloaked one', the immediate recipient of God's revelation (1). Traditions state that the transmission of the Qur'ān brought Muhammad considerable physical and emotional turmoil; this may be in part at least the import of its being a 'momentous' or weighty message (5). The prophetic experience begins with brokenness, and leads to a personal transformation issuing in a commitment to intensive religious practice which is shared with those who accept its teaching (6-7).

However, there is also a shadow side to the prophetic event, constituted by those who reject the divine message (11). God's response to such obstinacy is here addressed to two audiences. To the Prophet himself, there is given the promise that punishment is stored up for such behaviour (12-14). This is a promise which at the same time reassures him by confirming the authenticity of his prophecy and also sets the boundaries of his responsibility, since he is not himself being asked to serve as the agent of retribution. This word to Muhammad is immediately followed by a word directed to the rejecters, a reminder of the story of Pharaoh as an example of the inevitable punishment of disobedience (15-19). Thus past history is invoked to underline the immediacy of the challenge facing human beings in the present, with consequences for them reaching into the future.

The sūra concludes by returning to those who have accepted the prophetic message (20). This long final verse dates from a later period than the preceding parts of the sūra and has in focus a very differently situated Muslim community. It sets out a considerable mitigation of the devotional practices described in the first few verses, so that it has often been cited as an example of abrogation within the Qur'ān. What remains unchanged, however, is the merciful favour of God towards the faithful, and the rewards that he has prepared for them. The announcement of this beneficence to the faithful is as much a part of the prophetic responsibility as is the admonition of threats to the faithless.

1. This and the following sūra (74, *al-Muddaththir*, 'Wrapped') address Muhammad as a figure shrouded in a cloak. The precise context of this is unclear – it may refer to the Prophet getting ready to pray, or to sleep, or to leave his house – but in any case it betokens an experience of being selected as the recipient of divine revelation. A well-known *ḥadīth* states that after his first experience of receiving the Qur'ān, Muhammad returned home trembling to his wife Khadīja and said to her: *Zammilūnī, zammilūnī*, 'Cover me, cover me'.[29]

2-4. Praying through the night was an enthusiastic response of the early Muslims to divine revelation; tradition records that they exhausted themselves through lack of sleep as a result.[30] These verses represent a Makkan setting – the implication of verse 4b may be that that part of the Qur'ān which had been delivered by this point was short enough to be recited 'slowly and distinctly' during the night.

5. The adjective used of the message is *thaqīl*, 'heavy'. Some *ḥadīth* imply a physical meaning in this – at the Qur'ān's first revelation, Muhammad told Khadīja, 'The angel caught me and pressed me so hard that I could not bear it any more.'[31] While this experience belongs individually to Muhammad as prophet, *thaqīl* is also taken by commentators to imply the immense significance of the message for all human beings, as is implied by the translation 'momentous'.

6. The coming of revelation is associated with night in Islam – the first stage of prophecy for Muhammad was given in visions during his sleep, and this in turn led to his deliberate seclusion of himself (*taḥannuth*) on Mount Ḥirā' at night.

10. This verse reflects an early Makkan context, where the Muslim community responds with forbearance to the experience of harassment.

11. 'A little while' may mean the short remaining term of the unbelievers' lives, or it may point to the imminence of the Day of Judgement. Alternatively, the verse has been interpreted within a historical framework, as referring to the victory of Badr.[32]

12-14. The terrifying imagery used by these verses to warn of the Day of Judgement is a repeated motif in the early Makkan sūras.

15. Muhammad and Moses are both given the title 'messenger' – *rasūl*, one who is sent.

15-19. As in *Ṭā Hā* 20.9ff., the figure of Moses is cited as an earlier example of prophetic activity who validates the prophethood of Muhammad. Unlike that passage, which was addressed to Muhammad himself, this reminder is given directly to the unbelieving Makkans.

20. This long verse is generally agreed to be later than the rest of the sūra. The implication that the amount of the Qur'ān to be recited is now much longer than that envisaged in verses 2-4, the reference to 'fighting in God's way', and the careful specification of a number of different circumstances which would make extensive recitation of the Qur'ān difficult, all point to the Madinan period. The provisions of this verse provide an instance of abrogation (*naskh*) within one and the same sūra of the Qur'ān.[33]

Questions from the scriptures

Prophets in the Qur'ān are both the same as and clearly distinguished from other people; at the same time as their human status is emphatically insisted upon, their distinctiveness comes from their special appointment by God. In the Hebrew scriptures, while there are bands of prophets and something like an institutionalized 'prophethood' at royal shrines, there is also emphasis on the separateness of the true prophet as the one set apart by God. The New Testament speaks of distinct charisms for both prophets and apostles, yet all form members of the one body. Throughout the scriptures, in different ways, there is thus a tension between uniqueness and universality in the status of the prophets, particularly in their relationships to God. This tension poses questions to the faithful of both religions.

How far can 'ordinary' Christians and Muslims expect to share in the prophetic experience of encounter with God and entrustment with the divine Word? Is there an absolute difference of kind between prophetic spirituality and that of the rest of us, or is this a matter of degree? Are the prophets granted knowledge of God of a theologically or ontologically superior order to other humans, or are they entrusted only with 'need to know' information for the work in hand?

Again, given the connections that scriptural texts repeatedly make between the prophets' encounter with God and the troubling of their souls, questions also arise about the intensity of prophetic suffering compared to that of other humans. To what extent will we know the turmoil of the prophet's heart in our own religious lives? Is the rupturing of human relationships which marks so many prophetic biographies the result of a rigorous working out of a faithfulness to the divine Word to which all should adhere, or is it restricted to the specifically prophetic vocation?

In both Christianity and Islam, there are traditions of mysticism which in different ways chart a path by which the devout can attain to a closer knowledge of God. How do these patterns of spirituality relate to prophetic paradigms of encounter, and how does the ascesis which they require relate to the prophetic experience of disruption? More widely, what part can imitation of the prophets play in the devotion of Christians and Muslims?

A further question about the universality of the prophetic experience – whether in the sense of an experience in which all might in principle participate or in the sense that it somehow represents the experience of humanity as a whole – is sharply raised by the observation that those recognized as prophets are overwhelmingly men. Is maleness in some way a necessary or usual part of prophetic status, or are there prophetic women whose vocations are or were unrecognized? What part might gender play in shaping the formulation of the prophetic message?

The questions could be extended to cover issues of linguistic formation, cultural context, educational background, ethnic origin, and other markers of human diversity. Underlying them all is the issue of our identification with the prophetic figure: do we feel that their experience and vocation is continuous with our own, or do they seem to us entirely other and solitary in the path they tread?

Chapter 3

What is prophecy?

The words 'prophecy' or 'prophet' are used to refer to centrally important figures in the Qur'ān and in the Hebrew Bible – they also appear in the New Testament, though not with the same prominence. Yet it would be foolish to assume that the meaning of these terms is identical in these different contexts, as the following two detailed studies show. Wadad Kadi describes Qur'ānic prophecy as an 'institution', pointing particularly to its grounding in the concept of covenant. Ellen Davis's paper, by contrast, shifts the investigation of the phenomenon in the Hebrew scriptures from institution to individual, highlighting the intimacy of the prophet's relationship with God.

What is prophecy? Reflections on a Qur'ānic institution in history

Wadad Kadi

A scholar wishing to discover what the Islamic tradition has to say about prophecy, *nubuwwa*, has many options. He could go to the Qur'ān and its vast exegetical literature, to the sizable *ḥadīth* literature, to the numerous books on the 'proofs / signs of prophecy' (*dalā'il / 'alāmāt al-nubuwwa*), to the popular literature called the 'stories / tales of prophets' (*qiṣaṣ al-anbiyā'*), or to the works of some intellectuals who reflected on prophecy as it fits into their respective systems, be they philosophers like Ibn Sīnā, or theologian-Sūfīs like Ghazālī, or jurist-rationalists like Ibn Rushd; one might even seek an inspired overview of prophecy in Islamic thought in the work of the great Ibn Khaldūn. The field is wide. Given the limitation of time and the context of our meeting, I shall focus in my presentation on the nature of prophecy as it is delineated in the Qur'ān. While I will remain faithful to the Qur'ānic texts as I understand them, I will try to retain my independence regarding the structure of the Qur'ānic vision of prophecy, since this might be a useful way for the start of a discussion on the subject. Inevitably this means that I will have to be selective in both choice of texts and emphasis.

The Qur'ānic material on prophecy falls into two main categories: the nature of prophecy and the history of prophecy. The two are closely connected, but it is possible, indeed helpful, to discuss each of them separately.

As I see it, the most striking thing about the nature of prophecy as it is presented in the Qur'ān is that prophecy is envisioned as an institution. Now the word 'institution' can mean a number of things. It can mean an organization, establishment, foundation, or the like, devoted to promotion of a particular cause or programme, especially of a public, educational or charitable character; it can mean the building devoted to such work; it can mean a well established and structured pattern of behaviour or of relationships that is accepted as a fundamental part of a culture; it can mean any familiar, long established person, thing or practice – a fixture; and it can mean any established law or custom. Also an institution comes into existence only when somebody or some party institutes it, i.e. starts it, initiates it, inaugurates it, sets it up, establishes it, organizes it, sets it in operation, brings it into practice or use, creating posts or offices thereof. Overall, thus, we can say that an institution is a formal entity that is legally established by a person or a group, and is embodied in some recognizable physical form, for the promotion of a cause that aims at serving broadly the public good over a long period of time, during which it becomes a fixture and a fundamental part of a culture. Let us see how this understanding of institution applies to prophecy in the Qur'ān.

Perhaps the best way to start this investigation is to examine the two verses that talk about a certain covenant that God made with the prophets, the *mīthāq al-nabiyyīn*. In the first of these we read:

> And when we took (*akhadhnā*) from the prophets their covenant and from you (O Muhammad) and from Noah, Abraham, Moses, and Jesus son of Mary. And we took from them a solemn covenant (*mīthāqan ghalīẓan*).[1]

Here we have clearly a situation in which two parties, God on the one hand and five named prophets on the other, enter into a formal contract with each other that is binding to both of them. But there is a difference between the two parties, for one of them, God, initiates the contract (*akhadhnā*, we took) and defines it as it seems, while the other party, the five prophets, merely react to God's initiative. This aspect of the covenant is made much clearer in the second verse that discusses the same covenant, which reads:

> And when God took (his) covenant from the prophets (and said:) 'Behold that which I have given you of scriptures (*kutub*) and wisdom (*ḥikma*). Afterwards there will come to you a messenger confirming (*muṣaddiq*) that which you possess. You shall believe in him and you shall help him.' He said: 'Do you agree (*a'aqrartum*)? And will you take up my burden (which I lay upon you) in this (matter)?' They said: We agree (*aqrarnā*).' He said: 'Then bear you witness and I will be a witness with you.'[2]

Here the covenant situation is graphically dramatized: the two parties talk to each other. The first party makes an offer to the second, and the second accepts the offer – just like what happens in any binding contract. Furthermore, the words used by both parties indicate that the offer on the one hand and the acceptance on the other are strictly legal: 'Do you agree?' and 'We agree.' And in order to further emphasize the legally binding aspect of the contract, the concept of witnessing is introduced at the end of the verse, as is normally done in solemn contracts: both parties bear witness, testify, that they legally accept their contract to be obligatory for them. Prophecy, thus, now has two features of an institution: its being established by a party and its having a formal, legal character.

Another feature of an institution which is mentioned in both verses is its being embodied in a recognizable physical form, namely the prophets. Although the first verse mentions only five such 'key' prophets (Muhammad, Noah, Abraham, Moses and Jesus), it is clear from the second verse that the material embodiment of prophecy lies in all prophets, not some of them only. But the second verse offers a further physical form in which prophecy is embodied, namely the scriptures and wisdom. Whereas wisdom can be considered a characterization of the prophets and/or scripture, scripture must indicate an additional physical form in which prophecy is expressed, thus adding a dimension to its physical embodiment.

The second verse also points to another institutional feature of prophecy: its being a long-term, integrated project. Already from the first verse we see this temporal stretch, all the way from Noah to Muhammad. But the second verse makes this aspect even clearer, though in a subtle way. The prophets in general are addressed as a group which has been given scriptures and wisdom. Immediately thereafter, they are told that another messenger would come whom they must believe and support. But the most important thing about this prophet – presumably Muhammad, who has been mentioned as an addressee in the previous covenantal verse – is that he would 'confirm' that which the other prophets possess. What this means is that, though prophecy is composed of various people, prophets, they all carry in essence the same message, the one confirming the other. Thus prophecy has the feature of cohesive unity and continuity over a long duration, and this is a feature of an institution.

The two last features of an institution, promotion of a cause and serving the public good, are not clearly addressed in the two verses about God's covenant with the prophets, although there is a hint of the feature of serving the public good in the verse that immediately follows the second covenant verse, which reads:

> Then whosoever after this shall turn away they will be among the sinful (*min al-fāsiqīn*).[3]

By identifying those who do not heed the prophets' message as 'sinful', the verse implies that when the addressees of the prophets do heed the prophets' message they will not be sinful, i.e. they have a chance to be saved, which serves them well, and salvation, obviously, implies public welfare. But we shall return to this point later.

For identifying the cause which prophecy promotes, we have to look for verses other than the two verses of the prophetic covenant. This cause can be summed up in two points: divine mercy and the elimination of potential arguments by men on the Day of Judgement. As for mercy, we read: 'we are ever sending messengers . . . a mercy (*raḥma*) from your Lord';[4] the scripture sent with Moses is called a guide (*imām*) and a mercy,[5] as is the scripture sent with Muhammad;[6] and Jesus is called a mercy[7] and Muhammad is said to have been sent 'solely as a mercy to the world'.[8] The elimination of potential arguments on the Day of Judgement is more complex. In one verse we find a general statement about that, namely that messengers are sent 'in order that mankind shall have no argument (*ḥujja*) against God after the messengers'.[9] In other verses, the specific arguments that those who reject the messengers would produce on the Day of Judgement are cited. One such group would say: 'we have found our fathers (*ābā'anā*) following a religion and we are following their footsteps';[10] another would pronounce the same statement with a minor variation: 'We have found our fathers (*ābā'anā*) following a religion and we are guided by their footsteps';[11] and another would say: 'Enough for us is that wherein we found our fathers (*ābā'anā*)'.[12] In a different manner, Muhammad is asked to warn people whose fathers had not been warned 'so they were unaware/oblivious (*ghāfilūn*)'.[13] In sum, God has instituted prophecy out of mercy for people so that they will have no excuse on the Day of Judgement for having departed from what the prophets taught them.

Now, for any reader familiar with the Qur'ān, this last point cannot but ring a loud bell in his mind: there is another verse in the Qur'ān which also declares,[14] using the same key terms used here – 'our fathers' (*ābā'unā*), 'unaware' (*ghāfilīn*) – the elimination of the possibility that the non-believers should argue that they merely followed in their fathers' footsteps or that they were unaware/oblivious of what they should have done. What is most striking, however, is that the context of this verse has nothing whatsoever to do with prophets and prophecy. Rather, it is a carry-on of the preceding verse[15] which discusses a Qur'ānic covenant quite separate from the covenant between God and the prophets – the covenant between God and mankind. Although this covenant, unlike the other Qur'ānic covenants, is not specifically called a *mīthāq* in the Qur'ān, it has been taken by practically all exegetes to be *the* crucial Qur'ānic covenant, so much so that some of them referred to the time it was concluded as 'the day of the covenant (*yawm al-mīthāq*)'. It reads, together with the verse that follows it:

> And when your Lord brought forth from the children of Adam, from their loins, their seed, and made them testify touching themselves: 'Am I not your Lord?' They said: 'Yes, we testify' – lest you should say on the Day of Resurrection: 'We have been unaware of this,' or lest you should say: 'It is only that our fathers were polytheists of old, and we were their seed after them; would you destroy us on account of what the falsifiers did?'[16]

Like the covenant between God and the prophets, this covenant has a formal, legal structure, is initiated by God and responded to by man, is composed of the standard contractual offer (by God) and acceptance (by the children of Adam), and is made secure by bearing witness, thus indicating that the two parties involved in it take it to be binding. Now, the exegetes differed greatly in interpreting this covenant, as I have discussed it elsewhere, but the most predominant understanding of it places it in the pre-earthly existence of man on earth, hence the reference to it as the 'first' covenant or the 'primordial' covenant. According to this interpretation, God took all mankind from Adam's loins and asked them whether he was their Lord, and they all answered in the affirmative, bearing witness to their statement by touching themselves. God then put them back in Adam's loins. Thus, when each person of them is born on this earth later on, he is born with prior awareness that God is his Lord and he is God's servant. This awareness is what some exegetes call the *fiṭra*, or the natural disposition of man, and what made the Islamic tradition consider all men to be born Muslim. And, in fact, it is because of man's commitment to the worship of God in the primordial covenant that the verse that immediately follows the verse of the covenant declares that men have no excuse on the Day of Judgement to claim that they were not aware of God's place in the universe, or to attribute their sinfulness to their fathers, in whose footsteps they merely followed. The contracting of the covenant makes departing from God's way ultimately inexcusable.

But, why did this verse entertain the possibility that man, or some men, should depart from God's way in the first place, if all men are born aware of God and solemnly committed to his worship as their only Lord? The verse of the covenant provides no clue. Other verses of the Qur'ān, however, do, describing man as inconstant: anxious, fretful,[17] hasty,[18] weak[19] and, above all, forgetful.[20] It is at this point that prophecy comes to take its specific place in the Qur'ānic vision of the cosmic order: one of the functions of its carriers is 'reminding' people (*mudhakkir*)[21] and one of the names given to some of their scriptures is 'the Reminder', *dhikr*;[22] also *tadhkira*.[23] And with that the discussion of prophecy as an institution comes full circle. The primordial, universal covenant between God and mankind gave all men the opportunity to live a life on earth that ends with salvation in the hereafter. But this was not going to happen, as God knew, due to man's natural frailties, and the universal covenant could not come to the rescue because it is a one-time, unique affair – because it is not an institution. What was needed for man's rescue is a continuous, long-lasting and formal institution, embodied physically in figures and things that man can recognize in his earthly existence, and that serves man's general welfare. But such an institution could take place only if God, man's Lord and initiator of the failed universal covenant, willed to establish such an institution, for every institution needs one who brings it into practice, creating posts or offices thereof. And God, according to the Qur'ān, indeed willed to establish such a rescue institution, out of mercy to mankind, and he thus concluded a new covenant with a group of mankind, the prophets, who would be sent to men as messengers, accompanied with scriptures and wisdom, to remind them of their primordial covenant, should they have forgotten it, and indeed many of them would have. Thus was born the institution of prophecy, an establishment through which God gives man, because of his mercy, another opportunity for attaining salvation. This is a final opportunity for rescue, and thus no man can claim on the Day of Judgement that he was unaware of God's place in the universe or lay the blame for his error on his father.

Let me turn to the second category in which the Qur'ānic material on prophecy falls, namely the history of prophecy. The outline of this history is simple. Throughout human existence on earth, from Adam's time to Muhammad's, God selected prophets whom he sent to the various peoples of the earth. They fulfilled their charge, but their success was far from universal. Those who rejected them received punishment from God and those who accepted them were given prosperity on earth. On the Day of Judgement, the rejecters will receive eternal punishment in Hellfire, and the accepters will receive eternal life in paradise. Behind this simple framework, however, lies a host of broad, complex issues on prophecy emanating from the historical experience of the prophets on earth. Among these, the main ones are the difference between prophets and messengers, the selection of prophets, the differentiation between prophets, the proofs of true prophecy, the content of the prophetic message, the function of prophets, and the relationship between the prophets and the people. I will spend the remainder of the time assigned to me discussing these issues and shall close with a short conclusion.

The Qur'ān uses two main words to indicate the agents of prophecy: *nabī* (pl. *anbiyā*' or *nabiyyūn*) which means prophet, and *rasūl* (pl. *rusul*, or, less frequently, *mursal*, pl. *mursalūn*), which means messenger or apostle. The words are used interchangeably and clearly indicate two complementary functions (see below). There is a slight indication in the Qur'ān that messengers are more elevated than prophets, since the word 'messengers' always precedes the word 'prophets' when the two occur together in one verse[24] and certainly the former word occurs much more frequently in the Qur'ān than the latter. The Islamic exegetical traditions offered varying interpretations for this distinction, but the most prevalent is that a messenger comes necessarily with a scripture, whereas a prophet does not, or that a messenger brings a new *sharī'a*, religious law, whereas the prophet continues an old one.

In the Qur'ān, prophets and messengers are selected (*ijtabā, iṣṭafā*; less frequently *ikhtāra, iṣṭana'a*) solely by God, and he chooses whomever he wills[25] from the children of Adam,[26] although he does choose messengers also from the jinn[27] and uses his angels to act as messengers, too.[28] Given the spiritual affinity between them, the human prophets and messengers are presented in the Qur'ān as kin to, or descendants of, one another,[29] and their selection is considered a favour or a blessing (*ni'ma*).[30] Overall, they are intensely conscious of their essence as mortal human beings (*bashar, rijāl*) who have bodies, eat food, take wives and produce offspring, walk in the markets, and the like,[31] and they, including Jesus, never even try to transgress this essence and claim divinity for themselves or ask that they be worshipped, for these things belong to God alone.[32] God guides them to the straight path[33] and they, in turn, obey God, surrender to him, fear him, ask for his forgiveness, and rely on him.[34] They act faithfully[35] and are of the righteous.[36] In fact, according to the Qur'ān, they are so pious and so deeply aware of their proper place in the world vis-à-vis God that 'when the revelations of the Merciful are recited to them, they fall down, prostrating and weeping'.[37]

Still, the prophets occupy the highest rank in the scale of human groups in heaven, where they are followed by the truthful / saints (*al-ṣiddīqīn*), the martyrs and the righteous (*al-ṣāliḥīn*);[38] even on earth, all of them, the Qur'ān says, have been preferred by God above his creatures.[39] Whether there is distinction in rank between the prophets themselves is not as clear. In several places the Qur'ān states that God makes no distinction between his messengers.[40] But in one place, this distinction is clearly stated: 'And we have preferred some of the prophets above others (*wa laqad faḍḍalnā ba'ḍa l-nabiyyīna 'alā ba'ḍ*)';[41] and, in another, the same statement is repeated almost verbatim, but with a clarifying addition: 'some of them are those whom God spoke to, and some of them he exalted (above others) in degree (*wa rafa'a ba'ḍahum darajāt*); and we gave Jesus, son of Mary, clear proofs and we supported him with the holy spirit (*rūḥ al-qudus*)'.[42] The case of the preferred status of Jesus is clear in the verse. As for the preferred prophet whom God spoke to, the Qur'ān explains elsewhere that it is Moses.[43] The unidentified prophet who is described in the verse as 'exalted in degree' is probably Abraham, who is called God's 'friend' (*khalīl*).[44] Thus here we have three 'distinguished' prophets, so to speak. But, if we go back to the verse of God's covenant with the prophets that enumerates the participants in that 'solemn covenant', we find five named prophets, the three mentioned in the preference verse and Noah and Muhammad. Noah receives preference possibly because of his beginning a new chapter in human history following the flood; in a way, thus, he is analogous to Adam, the first Qur'ānic prophet, who started human history. As for Muhammad, there is no question whatsoever that he occupies a preferred status in the Qur'ān. He is given special privileges concerning marriage;[45] no one is allowed to marry his widows after his demise;[46] there are special regulations about entering his house;[47] people are commanded not to harm him[48] nor to raise their voices above his,[49] and are commanded to pray over him, as God and the angels do.[50] In addition, the Qur'ān also clearly gives Muhammad a special distinguished status among the prophets in two other verses which could easily be interpreted to mean that his sending as a messenger was annunciated in previous scriptures. In one of these,[51] Jesus tells the Children of Israel: 'I am God's messenger to you confirming what has been (revealed) before me in the Torah and bringing the good tidings of a messenger who comes after me whose name is *Aḥmad.' Aḥmad* is understood in the Islamic tradition as a clear reference to Muhammad. In the second,[52] Muhammad's messengership is included in the very verse that announces the general covenant between God and the prophets; there the people are asked to believe and help him: 'Afterwards there will come to you a messenger confirming that which you possess. You shall believe in him and you shall help him.' But most importantly, Muhammad is described in the Qur'ān as the 'seal of the prophets' (*khātam al-nabiyyīn*): 'Muhammad is not the father of any man among you, but he is the messenger of God and the seal of the prophets.'[53] This is a status granted to no other prophet in the Qur'ān. It has been variously interpreted as the last of the prophets, or the prophet who confirms the messages of the previous prophets. The first meaning is by far the most prevalent in the Islamic tradition. Those who accept it, though, do not deny the second meaning, for which there is ample proof in the Qur'ān.

The messengers chosen and honoured by God are said in the Qur'ān to be supported by clear proofs (*bayyina*; pl. *bayyināt*) of various kinds,[54] like miracles, scriptures, the balance, iron, and knowledge of the unseen.[55] But all the extraordinary actions undertaken by messengers are done only with God's permission;[56] did not Jesus, the greatest miracle worker, have this to say to the Children of Israel: 'I have come to you with a sign from your Lord, that I create for you out of clay like the form of a bird, then I breathe into it and it becomes a bird *with God's permission*; and I heal the blind and the leprous and bring the dead to life *with God's permission*'?[57] As for the scriptures, they originate from God and are imparted to the messengers through a process called *waḥy* (revelation) or *tanzīl* (sending down), as is so often repeated in the Qur'ān; indeed in two verses only,[58] we have the names of thirteen prophets who received revelation from God: Muhammad, Abraham, Ishmael, Isaac, Jacob, the tribes, Jesus, Job, Jonah, Aaron, Solomon, David and Moses. No details are given about the revelation process, except in the case of Moses, who, as we have seen before, was spoken to directly by God,[59] and in the case of Muhammad, where the revelation is described as 'sent down to your heart by God's permission' through the agency of the angel Gabriel;[60] Gabriel is also referred to in other instances as the 'Faithful Spirit' (*al-rūḥ al-amīn*)[61] and the Holy Spirit (*rūḥ al-qudus*).[62] In one verse,[63] the agency of an angel seems to be the standard way used by God to communicate his message through the prophets, and, in another,[64] the generic word 'veil' (*ḥijāb*) is used to indicate the impossibility of direct communication between God and man (except for Moses, of course). In a few cases, dreams act as a medium of communication between God and Abraham[65] and between God and Muhammad,[66] but in such cases no 'scriptural' revelation is involved. In the cases where scriptural revelations are involved, the revelations are normally called *kutub*, books (sg. *kitāb*), but some of these revelations are given specific names: the 'Torah' (*tawrāt*) is the name of Moses' book;[67] the 'Psalms' (*zabūr*) is David's;[68] the 'Gospel' (*injīl*) is Jesus';[69] and Muhammad's book gets several names: *Qur'ān, Furqān*, and *al-Kitāb*, and *Dhikr*, among others. A generic word used for some of the ancient scriptures is *ṣuḥuf*, meaning scrolls.[70]

The aim of the proofs provided by God to his prophets is to give credence and veracity to their respective prophecies. This is necessary in view of the fact that mankind could very well be exposed to one false prophet or another who 'forges a lie (*iftarā*) against God or says: It has been revealed to me (*ūḥiya ilayya*), when nothing was revealed to him, or one who says: I can bring down the like of what God has brought down'.[71] On the Day of Judgement, such unjust claimants 'are awarded doom of degradation for that which you spoke about God other than the truth'.[72] On another level, the prophets themselves are said in the Qur'ān to be subjected to the guiles of false 'inspirers' who act as if they were communicating to them revelations from God – *waswasa* (a word not used for true revelation) or *awḥā* (the main word used for true revelation). Such 'inspirers' – Satan (*al-shayṭān*) or the demons / devils (*shayāṭīn*), be they human or jinn – are meant to put the prophets to the test and deflect their attention so that they dispute with those creatures,[73] as it happened with the prophet Adam.[74] But this phenomenon, according to the Qur'ān, occurs not sporadically but to *every* messenger and prophet: 'Thus we have appointed to every prophet an adversary – devils of humankind or of jinn – who inspire (*yūḥī*) to one another plausible speech for the purpose of deceit (*ghurūran*).'[75] 'Never did we send a messenger or a prophet before you except when he recited (the message) the Devil proposed (opposition) in his recitation.'[76] The Qur'ān emphasizes that if God had not willed that the false inspirers do their adversarial work they would not have done so.[77] So the prophets must leave them alone to deceive the non-believers and make them earn their punishment in the hereafter.[78] As for the prophets and the believers, they know what comes from God and what does not;[79] after all, 'God abrogates what the Devil proposes, then God establishes his revelations.'[80]

The true prophets carrying the true message of God have been sent to all peoples of the earth,[81] to every town,[82] so that 'there is no people but' a messenger 'has passed among them'[83] and 'there is for every folk a guide';[84] Muhammad, in particular, is said to be sent to all mankind.[85] These messengers came in succession one after another,[86] so that they form an integral part of human history as perceived by the Qur'ān, and, in the tradition of institutions, can be viewed as recognizable fixtures of that history. Only one period of cessation (*fatra*) occurred between Jesus and Muhammad.[87] The Qur'ān mentions frequently the names of the messengers in a variety of sequences;[88] some of them (like Joseph and Jonah) have sūras named after them,[89] and there is a whole sūra dedicated to many of their stories entitled 'The Prophets' (*al-anbiyā'*).[90] Some of these prophets are known from the Bible (including Adam, Lot and Ishmael), but others (like Hūd and Ṣāliḥ) are not biblical and seem to be Arabian prophets. Numerous as the prophets mentioned in the Qur'ān are, the Qur'ān is clear that not all of those who were sent by God are mentioned there.[91] Further, in order that there be no ambiguity about people understanding the message brought to them by the prophets, the Qur'ān emphasizes that messengers are sent in the tongues of their respective peoples;[92] and this is one of the main principles underlying the Arabic character of the Qur'ān, mentioned several times.[93]

The content of the prophets' message testifies to their veracity. All messengers call people to accept as true exactly what they had committed themselves to accept as true on the 'day of the covenant', in primordial times, namely to worship God, the one true god, as their Lord,[94] the One to be worshipped and feared,[95] and, conversely, not to follow false gods.[96] More broadly, the message calls people to believe in God, his angels, scriptures and messengers, the messengers' various messages over time[97] and in the Day of Judgement.[98] The content of the messengers' message also includes cultic regulations, like

Abraham's instituting the pilgrimage; moral instruction, like ordering good and forbidding evil; precepts of social and political order, like adhering to justice symbolized by the balance;[99] and even, occasionally, instruction in matters that promote people's good, symbolized by iron.[100] It is important to keep in mind that, although the Qur'ān gives accounts of what various prophets said to their respective peoples, it does emphasize that all prophetic messages are essentially variations on the same theme, and thus we read this address to Muhammad:

> Say (O Muhammad): we believe in God and that which was revealed to us and that which was revealed to Abraham, Isaac, Jacob and the tribes, and that which was given to Moses, Jesus and the prophets from their Lord, we make no distinction between any of them, and unto him we have surrendered (*wa naḥnu lahu muslimūn*).[101]

This message constitutes what the Qur'ān calls the pure and true religion (*dīn*),[102] which is God's own.[103] And, since all messages are essentially one and the same, this religion, God's, is called 'Islam',[104] and in more than one instance it is described as the religion that shall prevail[105] and is identified as the only religion that God will accept.[106]

The Qur'ān identifies several functions for the prophets. The most fundamental is to convey God's message to the people accurately. This function is called *balāgh* in the Qur'ān,[107] and it is clear from several verses that it is meant primarily to absolve the prophets from responsibility in case people reject the message they preach[108] or, to a lesser extent, in case they die prematurely.[109] Indeed, if a messenger does not convey the message God chose him to convey, he would have forfeited his basic charge,[110] although this is unlikely to happen since, as we are told, God makes a guardian-angel walk before the prophets and messengers and behind them 'so that they may know that they have delivered (*ablaghū*) the messages of their Lord',[111] for which reason, we read: 'O messengers, I am aware of what you do.'[112] Another function of the prophets is to be reminders to the people, as is said of Muhammad,[113] and that means, according to the interpretation I have presented above, that they remind people of the primordial covenant they had made with God before they were born. This is why the scriptures revealed by God to the prophets are frequently given the name *dhikr*[114] or, less frequently, *tadhkira*,[115] as was noted before; both of these words are derived from the root *dh-k-r-*, whose meaning is 'to remember / remind'. But by far the two most common terms used in the Qur'ān for the function of the prophets are the two antonyms: *mubashshirūn* (sg. *mubashshir*; also *bashīr*, which is not used in the plural), meaning 'bringers of good tidings', and *mundhirūn* (sg. *mundhir*; also *nadhīr*, which is not used in the plural), meaning 'warners', and in most cases the two terms are paired together.[116] These two appellations point to the consequences that will befall the audiences of the prophets: those who believe them will be saved in the hereafter and therefore the prophets' message brings good tidings to them; and, conversely, those who reject them will be punished in the hereafter and therefore the prophets' message is a warning to them. Another function of the prophets is to adjudicate in the affairs of the people they are sent to when those people differ,[117] and they do actually pose as arbitrators (*ḥakam*): they use in making their judgements the revelations they have received[118] and they judge with equity.[119] Still another function attributed to the prophets in the Qur'ān is witnessing (*shāhid*, pl. *shuhadā'*). This term is used generally for Muhammad,[120] but in other instances of its usage, it is clear that this prophetic function is connected with the Day of Judgement: on that day, each prophet sent to each nation will be a witness to his own people.[121] It is not clear from the Qur'ān what exactly the prophets would do, as witnesses, to their respective peoples; the only thing which is fairly, though not fully, clear is that they cannot intercede for those of them who have rejected the message, even if they were their relatives and kin.[122] Even if a prophet tries to ask God for forgiveness for a relative, his request will be turned down. Thus we read about Muhammad: 'ask forgiveness for them or do not ask; if you ask forgiveness for them seventy times God will not forgive them. This is because they disbelieved in God and his messenger. God does not guide the wrongdoing folk.'[123]

The mission of the prophets and messengers is portrayed in the Qur'ān as a very thorny one, in which the likelihood of people accepting what the messengers call them to is a rarity. Indeed, most people would make the messengers' road difficult by asking the prophets for signs to support their claims,[124] or for a specific sign,[125] or reject the signs that they bring,[126] or even destroy these signs, as the people of Thamūd did with Ṣāliḥ's she-camel.[127] Indeed, it was after this incident with Ṣāliḥ's she-camel that God decided not to send any more signs.[128] Though he can certainly provide them, there is no use in doing so, for the people will not believe anyway.[129] Still worse, people would accuse the messengers of lying,[130] of being madmen,[131] sorcerers,[132] soothsayers,[133] poets,[134] or of recounting 'muddled dreams' (*aḍghāth aḥlām*)[135] or fables of the past[136] rather than true revelations, and they would ridicule them.[137] Things might get even worse for the prophets: their respective people could arrogantly threaten them with expulsion from the land,[138] with stoning[139] or with punishing them,[140] or could otherwise harm them,[141] or even wrongfully kill them.[142] Faced with such challenges, some prophets become distressed[143] but eventually take refuge in patience,[144] knowing that God will come to their rescue,[145] sometimes reminding them of the trials which their predecessors had to face. And together with God's rescue of them comes God's severe punishment of the non-believers in the prophets and messengers, their destruction in various ways and their replacement by other peoples, as is well known from the numerous 'punishment stories' in the Qur'ān. Indeed, this cyclical phenomenon of punishment followed by substitution is called the unchanging 'way of God' (*sunnat Allāh*),[146] and is one of the most conspicuous features of the Qur'ānic view of human history.

Let me wrap up with some concluding remarks.

The fundamental importance of the place of prophecy in the cosmic order envisioned by God for the sake of man in the Qur'ān cannot be overemphasized. In order to appreciate the vital nature of this place, one need only take a cursory look at the stages of human existence as they are portrayed there. In the Qur'ānic view, as I see it, there are four stages of human existence. The first is the Adamic stage in the Garden, which was tainted with the sin of disobedience but ended with forgiveness being granted to Adam. The second is the covenantal stage, in which a universal commitment was given by all men to God to worship him as their Lord and hence theoretically attain salvation. The third is the earthly stage in which most men, due to various weaknesses ingrained in them, broke their commitment to God and went astray, thus jeopardizing their chances of salvation. It is in this stage that God set in operation the institution of prophecy, out of mercy to men, sending one messenger after another and one scripture after another, in order that men have a new and final chance at eternal salvation. The reaction of men to this crucial institution will decide their fate in the fourth and final stage, the resurrectional stage, in which human existence comes full circle. During that stage, 'those who keep God's pact (*ʿahd Allāh*) and do not break the covenant (*al-mīthāq*)' are awarded heaven, and 'those who break God's pact after ratifying it (as a covenant; *min baʿdi mīthāqihi*)' are accursed and 'theirs is the ill abode'.[147] This is how critically important prophecy is in the Qur'ān. The only other institution that matches it in importance is the scriptures some prophets brought with them. In the case of Muhammad in particular, the scripture that was revealed through him – the Qur'ān – is especially important since it survives, as an expression of God's mercy, the demise of this 'seal of the prophets'.

'My devoted friend': The prophet as the intimate of God

Ellen F. Davis

As I thought about the question posed for this session – 'What is prophecy?' – I realized that the biblical writers are more interested in a slightly different kind of question, something like, 'Who is the prophet?', 'What is the prophet's experience of God?' My point is that the biblical writers are tremendously interested in a couple of dozen particular individuals known as *prophets*, but almost deliberately not interested in *prophecy* as such, although prophecy was a widespread social and political institution in the biblical world. We know from the Bible and other texts that ancient Near Eastern kings kept prophets on staff and also consulted independent visionaries in order to learn whether the gods were supporting their programmes, or whether they could be induced to do so. In Israel, too, prophets and kingship go together. While Abraham is at one point called a prophet[148] and Moses is a model for all prophets, it is only with the rise of the monarchy in the tenth century that we begin to hear about prophets in any numbers. It seems that gangs or 'schools' of prophets were found in the royal court, probably at royal sanctuaries and holy places scattered through the land, where the general population would also have consulted them. Yet the biblical writers tell us almost nothing about what most ancient Israelites must have thought of as 'prophecy' – that is, a social institution, with both royal support and public endorsement.

Indeed, the earliest biblical witness on prophecy, Amos in the eighth century, distances himself from exactly that understanding of prophecy-as-institution when he says, 'I am no prophet, nor am I a disciple of a prophet (*v^{e}lo ' ben-navī' 'anókhī*).'[149] Of course, he is not denying that he is God's true prophet. In fact, probably the earliest insight into how prophets experience God is Amos' assertion: 'My Lord GOD doesn't do a thing without divulging his privileged communication (*sōdō*) to his servants the prophets.'[150] The prophets are the servants of God, but equally, they are the confidants of God. They have 'stood in [God's] inner circle'[151] – again, the word is *sōd*, the privileged inner circle to whom God speaks directly, hiding nothing.

The prophets are the very few whom God actively seeks out and treats as intimates. In the Isaiah tradition, God calls Abraham, the progenitor of all prophets, *'ohavī*[152] – literally, 'my love', but since the word 'love' (in Hebrew, *'ahav*) is part of the diplomatic vocabulary of the ancient Near East, one might better render *'ohavī* as 'my devoted friend', 'my trusted ally'.[153] In the context of the biblical story, the term points to the fact that the two, God and Abraham, are bound together both by unguarded mutual devotion and by what you might call a shared life-project, namely fostering the faithfulness of the people Israel.

In this lecture I want to suggest that recognizing the intimacy that obtains between the prophet and God is important in three ways: first, it is key to understanding the words and experiences of the prophets as reported in the Bible. Second, it is an indispensable element of biblical theology. As we shall see, the prophet's intimacy with God sheds light on the complex interaction between divine anger and divine love, between justice and mercy. Third, the intimacy between God and the prophets may deepen understanding of the identity and work of Jesus, whom Christians believe to be the greatest of the prophets.

As with more ordinary relationships, intimacy grows where mutual trust is practised over time, and each partner proves reliable for the other. The most obvious evidence that God relies on the prophet is the commissioning of the prophet to speak for God. As God says to Jeremiah, 'I have put my words in your mouth.'[154] Many prophetic oracles are prefaced by the so-called 'messenger formula', 'Thus says YHWH.' Diplomatic messengers throughout the region used a similar authenticating marker: for instance, the imperial envoy Ravshakeh addressing the people of Judah, 'Thus says the King of Assyria.'[155] So the prophet uses the messenger formula to assert that he or (in one case) she[156] is no 'spin doctor'; God's message is delivered exactly as received, with no qualification or amelioration depending on the mood of the crowd.

Reciprocally, the prophet's utter reliance on God means that he seeks nothing for himself, putting his life totally at God's disposal. In other words, the prophet forfeits what we might consider the basic human right to ordinary experience. In so far as we know anything about the family life of any of the prophets, it never even approaches normality. God hijacks Hosea's marriage and turns it into a lived parable of God's own tragic covenant with Israel. Likewise, Isaiah's family life becomes an enacted message; he marries another prophet and gives his son a ridiculous name that points to political events unfolding on the international scene. (The poor child is named *Maher-Shalal-Hash-Baz*, Plunder-Is-Speedy-Looting-Comes-Fast.) As for Jeremiah, he has no family life at all. The message he conveys alienates his relatives; he remains unmarried and childless. The biblical record shows the prophet's range of experience reduced to the radical minimum; the word and the direct actions of God are the only stimuli to which he is allowed to respond freely. That drastic narrowing of the prophet's emotional life is most evident with Ezekiel, who by God's command is deprived of even the seemingly inescapable experience of mourning when his wife dies: 'Look, I am about to take away from you the delight of your eyes with a single blow, yet you shall not mourn or weep; there will be none of your tears. If you sigh, do it quietly; and don't observe mourning rites.'[157] That extraordinary prohibition casts into relief the public drama of mourning that God commands Ezekiel to enact when the divine sword is unsheathed against Jerusalem: 'Moan, with breaking loins and bitterness, moan before their eyes. And when they say, "Why are you moaning?", you shall say, "Over the news that has come; and every heart will melt and all hands will fall lax, and every spirit will grow faint and all knees will turn to water. Look, it is coming, and it will happen" – an utterance of YHWH.'[158]

Although the prophet's emotional life may be severely limited in range and expression, within one channel it is fiercely intense. Among modern scholars, the Jewish philosopher and theologian Abraham Joshua Heschel has characterized the prophet's emotional experience in most striking terms. He proposes that the Israelite prophet is above all the one who feels and shares the divine pathos – that is, the 'love and disappointment, mercy and indignation' felt by the God who is personally involved in the life of humankind and of Israel in particular. Heschel observes that 'the fundamental experience of the prophet is fellowship with the feelings of God, a *sympathy with the divine pathos* ... Sympathy is the prophet's answer to inspiration, the correlative to revelation ... The prophet hears God's voice and feels His heart.'[159]

But there is another side to prophetic sympathy: the prophet also feels keenly for his fellow Israelites. Although he cannot sympathize with their attitude of rebellion toward God, he shares in the pain of their failure; and that leads the prophet at times to stand over against God and oppose God's judgement against Israel. So the prophet is much more than a mouthpiece for the divine ventriloquist. While the prophetic books are dominated by messenger speeches, with the prophet speaking God's words, there are also numerous small narratives in which the prophet 'talks back' to God (in the strong sense of that phrase), objecting strenuously to the declared divine intention. We see that for the first time when Abraham argues presumptuously that it is unworthy of God to destroy Sodom and Gomorrah, if there are still a few decent folks left in the place: 'It is profanation to you (*halilah l^{e}khā*) to do something like this, to kill the righteous with the wicked, so the righteous fare just like the wicked. It is profanation to you! Shall not the Judge of all the earth do justice?'[160] The presumption to speak out against divine destruction is the measure of the prophet's identification with his people; but equally, it is the measure of his intimacy with God. For genuine intimacy does not mean sharing a single perspective on everything; indeed, total agreement is more likely to characterize a relationship of unhealthy subservience. By contrast, every truly intimate relationship allows and even encourages a degree of presumption, as we know from ordinary experience. We all trust certain people to presume on their intimacy with us; at times we actually rely on them to be aggressive in challenging our point of view.

In order to understand the function of the prophetic challenge to God, it is crucial to see that God only tolerates certain kinds of presumption from the prophet. Most notably, what is excluded is any expression of self-concern. Recall that Elijah flees from Jezebel, who is on a killing spree with the prophets of YHWH; and he runs all the way from Mount Carmel to the wilderness of Sinai (Horeb). Elijah sees himself as a second Moses, it seems; he is looking for some divine appreciation for his sufferings. And what does he get? Only God's impatient question, 'What are you doing *here*, Elijah?'[161] And then, in a classic show of divine sarcasm, God tells Elijah he's got the wrong 'wilderness', so to speak. 'Get on your way back to the wilderness of Damascus',[162] the foreign territory where God has real work for this prophet to do: two kings to anoint, and also Elijah's own prophetic successor Elisha – 'in your stead', God says.[163] No one is irreplaceable. A second example of prophetic self-pity expressed and excluded: Jeremiah complains to God about the endless pain of his vocation, and he's pretty rude about it: 'To me, you're like a waterhole that is dry when you need it most (*mayim lo' ne'^{e}manū*)!' God snaps right back: '*If* you say what is valuable instead of what is worthless, *then* you can be as my mouth.'[164] This is, you might say, a truly intimate exchange.

So God has zero-tolerance for prophetic self-pity. Yet it is a completely different story when the prophet speaks forcefully on behalf of Israel; then God listens and acts in direct response. Already with Amos, the prophet appears as a powerful intercessor, when God shows him a vision of doom for Israel, a plague of locusts consuming the whole year's crop of grain. Thus Amos reports that encounter: 'And when it had finished eating the green growth of the land, I said, "Lord GOD, forgive! How will Jacob survive? For he is so small." YHWH changed his mind about this. "It will not be," said YHWH.'[165] A second moment of prophetic challenge: 'Thus the Lord GOD showed me: here was the Lord GOD summoning [force] to contend by fire, and it consumed the great deep, and it was consuming the fields. And I said, "My Lord GOD, stop! How will Jacob survive? For he is so small." YHWH changed his mind about this. "This, too, will not be," said the Lord GOD.'[166]

Twice God relents. In the end, Amos' plea succeeds only in gaining time for Israel; and finally God says, 'I will not pass them by [harmlessly] any more.'[167] Nonetheless, the encounter sets the paradigm for the work of the prophet, who not only calls Israel to repentance but also pleads for her survival and sometimes is able to mitigate God's anger. But some prophets are not privileged to turn back God's wrath – especially Jeremiah and Ezekiel, who prophesy immediately before and during the fall of Jerusalem in 586 BCE and the exile of the people to Babylon. But still they try, and so it is noteworthy that these two are the prophets who protest most consistently against the divine decree. The distinctive rhetorical marker of that protest is the recurrent phrase, 'Ahah, my Lord GOD'.[168] I call it 'the covenantal protest'; in every case it denotes that the prophet is unresigned to what God either requires of him or intends for the people. Ezekiel's distraught cry is typical of the covenantal protest: 'Ahah, my Lord GOD, are you going to destroy the whole remnant of Israel as you pour out your wrath on Jerusalem?'[169]

Another passage in Ezekiel indicates that God not only tolerates such a protest on behalf of the people but indeed, actively solicits it. God is lamenting the 'conspiracy of [false] prophets'[170] who soothe Israel with phoney oracles of *shalōm*, peace and prosperity;[171] and God gives this astonishing account:

> I sought among them someone to shore up the wall or stand in the breach before me on behalf of the land, so I might not destroy it; but I found no one. So I poured out my indignation on them; with the fire of my rage I finished them off.[172]

It is an amazing statement about the dynamics of divine jurisprudence within the context of covenant: God the Just Judge seeks out the best defence counsel, a faithful prophet competent to deflect the divine decree from the guilty people. But this system of checks and balances fails: 'I found no one.' For too long the false prophets held the attention of the people; at a crucial time, they overshadowed the true prophet. And so God's apparent desire for leniency cannot prevail, and the judgement proceeds as decreed.

But the legal analogy only goes so far. The sending of the prophets represents more than a divine nod to Israel's 'constitutional' right to a proper defence. It is more than a matter of theodicy, of God's justice. Rather, as Yochanan Muffs says, in his wonderful study of prophetic intercession: 'God originally sent prophets to Israel to demonstrate to them His great love. Even at the moment of His anger, He manifests His love by listening to the prayers of the prophets, prayers that control and calm His anger.'[173] Divine love actively seeking opposition to divine wrath – that paradox is developed in a *midrash* that dramatizes the moment when Moses appears before God to hand over his soul in death. Of course, the rabbis turn to Moses to explain the peculiar partnership formed between God and the prophet for Israel's sake. More than any other biblical account, the story of Moses gives us insight into the prolonged intimacy between God and a human being; and as it turns out, that relationship involves a fair amount of wrangling. As Muffs observes, 'Moses' whole life was a battle of words, his attempt to prevent the anger of the Lord from destroying the people.'[174] Already at Sinai, after they had sinned in worshipping before the Golden Calf, God decided to kill these Israelites off and start all over again – just God and Moses – and make a new people. But Moses 'sweetened God's face';[175] he mollified God with what, were it any other interlocutor, we would call a clever psychological ploy: 'What will the Egyptians say?'[176] Now, forty years later, Moses is at the point of death; and as the rabbis imagine the scene, God is grief-stricken and deeply anxious – not that Moses might be eternally lost to God (that seems impossible), but that Israel might be. So, the account goes, 'God said, Who will stand against me on the day of wrath?[177] This means, Who shall protect Israel in the hour of My anger? And who will stand up in the great eschatological war for My children? And who will speak up for them when they sin against Me?'[178]

'The great eschatological war for My children' – the phrase suggests that the intercessory role of the prophet is not confined to helping the people and the kings of Israel negotiate the complexities of their *political* existence. Prophets and kings often go together in the Bible, as I have said. Yet Moses is needed to intercede for the Israelites already at Sinai, as soon as they are consecrated as God's people, long before they have a land or a king. Thus we may infer that the prophetic function of intercession does not cease when the House of David collapses. A faithful intercessor is needed as long as the people Israel endures, a fallible people standing before the Righteous Judge who, as the Psalmist says, 'has indignation every single day'.[179] Although the last few centuries of the biblical period added little to the preserved prophetic tradition, and early rabbinic Judaism affirmed that scribal religion had superseded prophecy as carrier of the divine spirit,[180] nonetheless both Jews and Christians continued to meditate on the role of the intercessor: the one who, being intimate with God, yet dares to speak out for the sinful people.

It is noteworthy that the medieval rabbis criticized the prophet Elijah precisely because they judged him to be an inadequate intercessor. The *midrash* represents Elijah as a religious fanatic who is overly critical of his own people's weakness: 'I am extremely zealous for YHWH God of Hosts, for the Israelites have abandoned your covenant, torn down your altars, and killed your prophets with a sword.'[181] So Elijah tattles on the people instead of defending them before God. Therefore the *midrash*, building on the biblical censure of Elijah, shows an ironic role reversal: God defends the people before Elijah. One story tells that there were in Elijah's time '365 pagan temples in Damascus, where each god had his day to be worshiped. There was one special day when all of them were worshiped together. On that day, God said to Elijah, "Before you start criticizing my children, go to Damascus and criticize them [the worshippers of 365 gods]!" '[182] The implication is that even among true prophets, some perform a greater service to God and the people. The greatest of the prophets are those who know the power and the necessity of intercessory prayer.

The gospels represent Jesus as the fulfilment of prophecy, as the greatest of the prophets and 'more than a prophet'.[183] It would seem that the dominant element of the prophetic paradigm, as the evangelists see it fulfilled in Jesus, is the prophet as mediator of divine power and bearer of the divine Word, whose message is rejected, and he is persecuted and killed for speaking God's truth.[184] But I believe the prophetic role I have highlighted here – the prophet as intercessor, who by reason of faithfulness and intimacy with God is qualified to plead for a people whose own voice is muted and distorted by sin –

this role of the prophet is also fulfilled in Jesus, and most evidently at the cross. For that is above all others the place where Jesus 'stands in the breach before [God]'[185] and intercedes for his own sinful people: 'Father forgive them, for they do not know what they are doing.'[186] The appeal of the criminal crucified at Jesus' side – 'Remember me when you come into your kingdom'[187] – is an appeal to Jesus as heavenly King, but also as the One who, being God, yet pleads for the sinful before God.

From this perspective, it is more evident why Christians claim that the cross is the fulfilment of Jesus' prophetic ministry. Jesus is killed for speaking God's truth, but that in itself is more consequence than fulfilment. It is a consequence of his fulfilment of the role of faithful messenger – indeed, a predictable consequence, since it had happened to many before him. What is fulfilled, perfected on the cross, is Jesus' ministry as prophetic intercessor, when through his death he makes fully effective intercession 'in the great eschatological war for [God's] children'.

Chapter 4

Sent to humanity

While the prophetic impulse has its origins in an encounter with God, it has to find its expression in relation to human beings organized in societies. As the four texts discussed in this chapter severally illustrate, the communication of God's Word is not a consensual or painless operation. On the contrary, it is likely to be strongly contested, to generate divisions between people, and to be personally costly for the messenger himself. In the rupture of human relationships by the divine Word, prophet and people alike face a stark challenge to adhere faithfully to the cause of God.

Scripture dialogue III

Hūd 11.25-49; Jeremiah 26

The two passages presented here describe the insertion of the prophetic word into social contexts in which it both creates conflicts, and also becomes a point around which conflicts cluster. The differing ways in which both the prophetic figures, and the God they serve, relate to those conflicts are presented through the differing dynamics of the two narratives. The biblical text, as compared to the Qur'ānic, seems to show a greater enmeshment of the prophetic event in the vortices of conflict.

Hūd 11.25-49

These verses from the sūra *Hūd* form one of several Qur'ānic passages telling of the intervention of the prophet Noah in the society of his time, and describing the events which led to a punitively destructive inundation of the world by God.[1] In the Qur'ānic account, this episode is seen as very much a story of division and contest between those who heed God's Word and those who scorn it. This is a sūra from the later Makkan period, which also includes references to the prophets Hūd (after whom it is named), Ṣāliḥ, Abraham, Shuʿayb and Moses. At a time when Muhammad and his followers were experiencing increasing persecution in the years leading up to the climactic event of the Hijra, the message directed to the Prophet in Makka is that these examples of past prophets contending with conflict should help to 'make firm his heart'.[2] As a counterpart to this encouragement, the divine address to the unbelieving peoples of past and present is consistently admonitory in tone.

Qur'ānic text

[25]We sent Noah to his people to say, 'I have come to you to give a clear warning: [26]worship no one but God. I fear for you that you may suffer on a painful Day.' [27]But the prominent disbelievers among his people said, 'We can see that you are nothing but a mortal like ourselves, and it is clear to see that only the vilest among us follow you. We cannot see how you are any better than we are. In fact, we think you are a liar.' [28]He said, 'My people, think: if I did have a clear sign from my Lord, and He had given me grace of His own, though it was hidden from you, could we force you to accept it against your will? [29]My people, I ask no reward for it from you; my reward comes only from God. I will not drive away the faithful: they are sure to meet their Lord. I can see you are foolish. [30]My people, who could help me against God if I drove the faithful away? Will you not take heed? [31]I am not telling you that I hold God's treasures, or have any knowledge of what is hidden, or that I am an angel. Nor do I say that God will not grant any good to those who are despised in your eyes: God Himself knows best what is in their souls. If I did this I would be one of the wrongdoers.' [32]They said, 'Noah! You have argued with us for too long. Bring down on us the punishment you threaten us with, if you are telling the truth.' [33]He said, 'It is God who will bring it down, if He wishes, and you will not be able to escape. [34]My advice will be no use to you if God wishes to leave you to your delusions: He is your Lord and to Him you will be returned.'

[35]If [these disbelievers] say, 'He has made this up,' say [Muhammad], 'If I have made this up, I am responsible for my own crime, but I am innocent of the crimes you commit.'

[36]It was revealed to Noah, 'None of your people will believe other than those who have already done so, so do not be distressed by what they do. [37]Build the Ark under Our [watchful] eyes and with Our inspiration. Do not plead with Me for those who have done evil – they will be drowned.' [38]So he began to build the Ark, and whenever leaders of his people passed by, they laughed at him. He said, 'You may scorn us now, but we will come to scorn you: [39]you will find out who will receive a humiliating punishment, and on whom a lasting suffering will descend.' [40]When Our command came, and water gushed up out of the earth, We

said, 'Place on board this Ark a pair of each species, and your
own family – except those against whom the sentence has
already been passed – and the believers,' though only a few
believed with him. 41He said, 'Board the Ark. In the name of God
it shall sail and anchor. My God is most forgiving and merciful.'
42It sailed with them on waves like mountains, and Noah called
out to his son, who stayed behind, 'Come aboard with us, my
son, do not stay with the disbelievers.' 43But he replied, 'I will
seek refuge on a mountain to save me from the water.' Noah
said, 'Today there is no refuge from God's command, except for
those on whom He has mercy.' The waves cut them off from
each other and he was among the drowned.
44Then it was said, 'Earth, swallow up your water, and sky, hold
back,' and the water subsided, the command was fulfilled. The
Ark settled on Mount Judi, and it was said, 'Gone are those evildoing people!' 45Noah called out to his Lord, saying, 'My Lord,
my son was one of my family, but Your promise is true, and You
are the most just of all judges.' 46God said, 'Noah, he was not one
of your family. What he did was not right. Do not ask Me for
things you know nothing about. I am warning you not to be
foolish.' 47He said, 'My Lord, I take refuge with You from asking
for things I know nothing about. If you do not forgive me, and
have mercy on me, I shall be one of the losers.' 48And it was said,
'Noah, descend in peace from Us, with blessings on you and on
some of the communities that will spring from those who are
with you. There will be others We will allow to enjoy life for a
time, but then a painful punishment from Us will afflict them.'
49These accounts are part of what was beyond your knowledge
[Muhammad]. We revealed them to you. Neither you nor your
people knew them before now, so be patient: the future belongs
to those who are aware of God.

Commentary

The story of Noah in this sūra follows on from a message of encouragement addressed by God to Muhammad in the disputes he was facing with the unbelieving Makkans (11.1-24). In those disputes, the key points at issue were the authenticity of the message claimed as revelation, and the qualifications of the messenger to be recognized as a genuine recipient of revelation. It is these very themes which echo in the account of Noah's dispute with the unbelievers of his time (27-31), making the moral of this example clear: as God vindicated Noah so he will vindicate Muhammad. At two points, the passage in fact swings forward in time to the Makkan situation as it turns to address Muhammad directly (35,49).

The narrative of Noah develops in three stages. The description of his altercation with his unbelieving compatriots (25-39) focuses on the prophet's credibility and his audience's response; as Noah's mode of prophecy here is emphatically admonitory in tone, what is at stake is on one hand the reality of the punishments of which he warns, and on the other hand the ability of his hearers to respond appropriately to these threats. Two clear limits are set to the prophet's activity in this dispute: he is not to be charged with responsibility for enacting retribution which belongs to God alone (33), and he cannot compel assent to the divine message from those who are faithless (28).

The conclusion of this section comes in God's explanation that further argumentation is futile as he has now decided on the destruction of the wicked (36-7). The narrative then continues with an account of the Flood, bringing the destruction of most and the salvation of a few. At this point, the text clearly echoes biblical and extra-biblical motifs, while also displaying significant differences from them (40-44). The theme particularly emphasized in this Qur'ānic account is that of the rupture brought by the divine punishment of evildoing. There have already been hints of the pain brought to the prophet by this conflict in the way he addresses his incredulous auditors as 'my people', but the sharpness of this pain is accentuated in the third and final part of the narrative, where Noah engages in a dialogue with God over the fate of his own son (45-8). The priority of faith over family is here asserted in uncompromising terms, to the extent that God creates a new genealogy for Noah which omits the unbeliever, even to the point of specifically rebuking the prophet for interceding for his son.

26. *Nūḥ* 71.23 specifies that the false gods whose worship has led astray Noah's compatriots are named Wadd, Suwa', Yaguth, Ya'uq and Nasr, deities of pre-Islamic Makka.

27. *Bādiya al-ra'yi*, an exercise of opinion which rapidly comes to a conclusion, is in this translation referred to the unbelievers: their assessment of the lowly status of Muhammad's followers seems to them clearly founded. It could also be a description of the faithful in the opinion of the unbelievers: 'their capacity is limited by hasty or immature judgement'.[3]

28-30. The repeated expression *qawmi*, 'my people', which Noah uses to address his audience emphasizes the natural bonds of kinship and society which attach him to them – and so also underlines the poignancy of the rupture which the prophetic word brings.

28. Noah's preaching explicitly recognizes the impossibility of coercing assent

to the divine revelation, even though this is described as issuing from God's grace (*raḥma*).

31. Noah's protests echo the dispute of Muhammad with his Makkan contemporaries, referred to earlier in this sūra. There, one of the complaints brought against the Prophet had been this: 'Why is no treasure sent down to him, why has no angel come with him?'[4] Such a question seems to suppose a magical or shamanistic understanding of the nature of revelation; true prophecy in Islamic terms, however, rests for its authentication on the inimitability of its message and on the confirmatory (in this case, punitive) action of God.

32-3. Despite his audience's challenge to exercise control himself over the consequences of their unbelief, Noah insists on the limitation of prophetic power and responsibility: his role is to admonish, but the actual delivery of retribution is reserved to God.[5]

33. From this verse onwards, the mood of confrontation perceptibly sharpens – the prophet no longer addresses his audience as 'my people' (*qawmi*).

35. Commentators generally regard this verse as being addressed directly to Muhammad, rather than Noah; like his predecessor, he is reminded and reassured that he is not himself responsible for the composition of the revealed divine Word which he transmits.

36-7. This decisively damnatory word, with its forbiddance of prophetic intercession, corresponds to the point in the biblical narrative at which God judges the corruption of the earth to be so severe that only its destruction will suffice.[6]

40-44. The narrative here has some obvious points in common with the biblical narrative in Genesis 7.6–8.5: for example, Noah and his family are saved; the species are taken onto the ark in pairs; water gushes up from the earth itself; the ark floats higher than the mountains; at the end, it rests on a mountain.[7] At the same time, there are also striking differences: one of Noah's sons is lost according to the Qur'ān, while on the other hand the Genesis narrative is far more detailed in the dimensions it specifies for the ark, the detailed chronology of the flood, the long account of Noah's experiments to test for the retreat of the waters, and so on. The two accounts can be read as different presentations of a more widespread tradition of a great inundation reaching back through the cultures of the ancient Near East.[8] What is significant is the way in which the Qur'ān accentuates those punitive and conflictual elements in the story which best serve its exemplary function in prophetic history.

45-8. Noah has to accept the division within his family caused by the prophetic message which his son failed to accept – exacerbating and making more intimate the disruption with his compatriots already hinted at earlier (verses 28-30).

The phrase *'innahu 'amal ghayr ṣāliḥ*, translated as 'what he did was not right', is here referred to the actions of Noah's son. It is also possible to read it, though, as applying to Noah's prayer on behalf of his son.[9] If this interpretation is followed, the sharpness of God's rebuke to Noah becomes clearer, as does the rupture effected with his physical offspring. The prohibition of further intercession mirrors, albeit in the opposite generational direction, a similar word addressed to Abraham about his unbelieving father.[10] New genealogies are provided for the prophets, to emphasize the priority for them of belief over kinship.

49. Whatever elements of the Noah story may be found within the ambient

culture, God insists that its true significance, as a making apparent of the unseen world (*al-ghayb*), can be known only through revelation (*waḥy*).

Jeremiah 26

Jeremiah 26 is set at the beginning of a cycle of stories which weave together Jeremiah's delivery of divine oracles in a troubled and divided Jerusalem, the various reactions to his interventions of the different groups in the city, and the effects of all this on the prophet's own life. This narrative may have been shaped by the scribe Baruch, who acted as Jeremiah's amanuensis; its third person form lends it something of a spirit of detachment as it describes how the prophetic event becomes immersed in, and in some ways exacerbates, the conflicts inherent in the situation. Yet this cannot be read simply as a disinterested historical account: the purpose of the chapter is to invite reflection on the present challenge of responding to God's Word.

Biblical text

> 1At the beginning of the reign of King Jehoiakim son of Josiah of
> Judah, this word came from the Lord: 2Thus says the Lord: Stand
> in the court of the Lord's house, and speak to all the cities of
> Judah that come to worship in the house of the Lord; speak to
> them all the words that I command you; do not hold back a
> word. 3It may be that they will listen, all of them, and will turn
> from their evil way, that I may change my mind about the dis-
> aster that I intend to bring on them because of their evil doings.
> 4You shall say to them: Thus says the Lord: If you will not listen
> to me, to walk in my law that I have set before you, 5and to heed
> the words of my servants the prophets whom I send to you
> urgently – though you have not heeded – 6then I will make this
> house like Shiloh, and I will make this city a curse for all the
> nations of the earth.
>
> 7The priests and the prophets and all the people heard Jeremiah
> speaking these words in the house of the Lord. 8And when
> Jeremiah had finished speaking all that the Lord had com-
> manded him to speak to all the people, then the priests and the
> prophets and all the people laid hold of him, saying, 'You shall
> die! 9Why have you prophesied in the name of the Lord, saying,
> "This house shall be like Shiloh, and this city shall be desolate,
> without inhabitant"?' And all the people gathered around
> Jeremiah in the house of the Lord.

[10]When the officials of Judah heard these things, they came up
from the king's house to the house of the Lord and took their
seat in the entry of the New Gate of the house of the Lord.
[11]Then the priests and the prophets said to the officials and to all
the people, 'This man deserves the sentence of death because he
has prophesied against this city, as you have heard with your
own ears.'
[12]Then Jeremiah spoke to all the officials and all the people, saying, 'It is the Lord who sent me to prophesy against this house
and this city all the words you have heard. [13]Now therefore
amend your ways and your doings, and obey the voice of the
Lord your God, and the Lord will change his mind about the
disaster that he has pronounced against you. [14]But as for me,
here I am in your hands. Do with me as seems good and right to
you. [15]Only know for certain that if you put me to death, you
will be bringing innocent blood upon yourselves and upon this
city and its inhabitants, for in truth the Lord sent me to you to
speak all these words in your ears.'
[16]Then the officials and all the people said to the priests and the
prophets, 'This man does not deserve the sentence of death, for
he has spoken to us in the name of the Lord our God.' [17]And
some of the elders of the land arose and said to all the assembled
people, [18]'Micah of Moresheth, who prophesied during the reign
of King Hezekiah of Judah, said to all the people of Judah: "Thus
says the Lord of hosts,
Zion shall be ploughed as a field;
    Jerusalem shall become a heap of ruins,
    and the mountain of the house a wooded height."
[19]Did King Hezekiah of Judah and all Judah actually put him to
death? Did he not fear the Lord and entreat the favour of the
Lord, and did not the Lord change his mind about the disaster
that he had pronounced against them? But we are about to bring
great disaster on ourselves!'
[20]There was another man prophesying in the name of the Lord,
Uriah son of Shemaiah from Kiriath-jearim. He prophesied
against this city and against this land in words exactly like those
of Jeremiah. [21]And when King Jehoiakim, with all his warriors
and all the officials, heard his words, the king sought to put him
to death; but when Uriah heard of it, he was afraid and fled and
escaped to Egypt. [22]Then King Jehoiakim sent Elnathan son of
Achbor and men with him to Egypt, [23]and they took Uriah from
Egypt and brought him to King Jehoiakim, who struck him

down with the sword and threw his dead body into the burial place of the common people.

[24]But the hand of Ahikam son of Shaphan was with Jeremiah so that he was not given over into the hands of the people to be put to death.

Commentary

This chapter describes Jeremiah as a prophet seeking to deliver faithfully the Word of God, and to elicit a change in his people's behaviour in response to that word, within a situation of suspicion, tension and internal conflict. In the already divided city of Jerusalem, the advent of the prophetic message has the immediate effect of adding to the divisions among the people, for Jeremiah is not here simply persecuted by an entire society: some take his side, others oppose him (8,16). Nevertheless, there is no sense that his oracles are being heeded by anybody in the way that their divine originator intends them. There is no great act of repentance as in previous years (19), and the city's condition at the end of the chapter is no better than at the beginning.

The unresolved state of Judah's fortunes is mirrored both in the uncertain predicament of the prophet and even, to some extent, in the apparent ambiguity of the divine purpose which he is to communicate. Jeremiah himself, while commissioned by God as messenger, relies for his protection on his ability to sway the minds of the people (15), and still more on the personal protection of a powerful official (24). There is no clear sense of a divinely guarded emissary set over and against his society; rather, the prophet is very much bound up with the complexities and tensions generated by the conflicts around him. The contrast with the martyred Uriah, whose fate is summarily spelt out at the end of the chapter (20-23), is remarkable.

Set against the sequence of prophetic history, the immediate disposition of God can also seem hard to discern. In one sense, of course, there is no ambiguity: within that history, Israel's God has delivered *tōrah* to his people, reminded them to adhere to it through the ministry of the prophets, and now sends Jeremiah with a still more urgent message of admonition (4-5). However, precisely because it is conditional on the people's response, God's attitude cannot at present be discerned; he 'may change his mind' (3,13) about the disaster he plans, but this cannot be presumed. The God who speaks into this situation of conflict seems himself to be rent by an internal struggle.

1. Jehoiakim became King of Judah in 609, when Jerusalem was under sustained pressure from the Babylonian empire.

2. The formula 'Thus says the Lord' (*kōh amar yhwh*) characterizes prophetic oracles in the Hebrew scriptures, marking them off as distinct from the human speech of the prophets.

2-6. Jeremiah's sermon in the Jerusalem temple corresponds to the longer oracle recorded in Jeremiah 7.1-15, and may represent the scribe Baruch's summary of the latter.

3. While Jeremiah's tone is relentlessly admonitory, he here holds out to his hearers the prospect of a more positive divine attitude consequent upon their repentance – a possibility repeated in verse 13.

4-5. Jeremiah does not bring any new instruction from God; on the contrary, the *tōrah* or instruction necessary for Israel has been clearly delivered already, and repeated by the sequence of prophetic messengers.

6. Shiloh, the northern sanctuary, had been destroyed long ago.[11] Jeremiah predicts a similar doom for both the spiritual ('this house') and the secular ('this city') life of Jerusalem.

7-9. It can be assumed from the text that the 'priests and prophets' were responsible for leading the opinion of 'all the people'. It is a recurring irony in the prophetic literature that those officially responsible for the maintenance of God's worship and the delivery of his word are those who resist his message.

10. The 'officials' (or 'princes', *sārīm*) of Judah are not necessarily or uniformly hostile to Jeremiah; it appears from the rest of the book that included among them are both opponents and supporters of his. Their function here is to constitute a court (meeting 'in the gate').

11. It is not clear on the basis of what charge a death sentence is demanded. One possible indictment is treason: it is 'against this city' that Jeremiah has prophesied, and that at a time of war. Another is falsely proclaiming his own opinions as the word of the Lord.[12]

12-13. Jeremiah defends himself against accusations of both treason and false prophecy: it is the Lord whose word he speaks, and if that word is heeded the city will benefit as a result.

16. The degree of acceptance of Jeremiah by the 'officials and all the people' should not be overestimated. Certainly his right to speak as a prophet is defended, and he is therefore acquitted of a capital crime. This does not mean, however, that the content of his message is affirmed as true, let alone that it is acted on.

17-19. The 'elders of the land', recalling prophetic history, cite the precedent of Micah, whose oracle was taken as a catalyst for repentance rather than a pretext for suppressing prophecy.[13] However, no repentance from the citizens of Jerusalem does in fact follow the elders' intervention; this episode, like that which follows it, is introduced to highlight the contrast between the godly rule of Hezekiah and the fickleness of Jehoiakim.

20-23. The figure of Uriah is difficult to interpret in terms of the theology of the book of Jeremiah.[14] It would be possible to see him as somebody who claimed to speak in the name of the Lord, following the example of Jeremiah but without his divine commissioning; his bloody fate in that case would be a deserved punishment for his presumption. However, the text lays great stress on the fact that his message was 'in words exactly like those of Jeremiah', and this seems difficult to reconcile with such an interpretation. A more plausible way of reading the text is to see it as contrasting, not Uriah with Jeremiah, but Jehoiakim with Hezekiah (as in verse 19); unlike his righteous predecessor, this king shamefully killed a messenger from the Lord – who should therefore be counted as a martyr. This reading would then call for an explanation of why Jeremiah did not meet a similar fate – and this is provided in explicitly non-theological terms in the following verse.

24. A remarkable feature of the narrative sections of the book of Jeremiah – clearly instanced in this verse – is the way in which they give 'secular' interpretations of the hero's fate. There is here no suggestion that God is himself guarding the life of his prophet – it is through the human agency of Ahikam that Jeremiah is preserved.[15] All this stands in tension with Jeremiah's own assurance of a protecting divine presence with him.[16]

Scripture dialogue IV

1 Kings 21; *al-Shu'arā'* 26.123-91

The two passages discussed here both describe prophetic interventions addressed to societies which have become radically disoriented from the will of God, and deeply corrupted as a result. Failure to heed the prophetic warning is liable to result in catastrophic consequences: in the four Qur'ānic examples, such fates are indeed enacted, while the Ahabite monarchy in Israel wins a temporary reprieve through a measure of repentance. In both cases, the respective scriptures present the Word of God as a critical standard against which the existing social order is judged, and as a powerful spiritual force which will bring about that order's destruction.

1 Kings 21

1 Kings 21 forms a part of the cycle of stories of the northern prophets Elijah and Elisha which have been embedded in a later account of the Israelite and Judaean kingdoms compiled and edited by a southern historian.[17] This editorial framework judges the royal history against the standard of God's *tōrah*, and finds it repeatedly lacking, particularly in the northern kingdom. In this chapter, the contest of prophet and monarch is expressed in a sharply drawn confrontation over a shocking abuse of royal power which is in direct contradiction to the divine plan for society. The dire consequences for the royal family of this confrontation will see their outworking later in the First and Second Books of Kings.[18]

Biblical text

[1]Later the following events took place: Naboth the Jezreelite had
a vineyard in Jezreel, beside the palace of King Ahab of Samaria.
[2]And Ahab said to Naboth, 'Give me your vineyard, so that I may
have it for a vegetable garden, because it is near my house; I
will give you a better vineyard for it; or, if it seems good to you,
I will give you its value in money.' [3]But Naboth said to Ahab,
'The Lord forbid that I should give you my ancestral inheritance.' [4]Ahab went home resentful and sullen because of what
Naboth the Jezreelite had said to him; for he had said, 'I will not
give you my ancestral inheritance.' He lay down on his bed,
turned away his face, and would not eat.
[5]His wife Jezebel came to him and said, 'Why are you so
depressed that you will not eat?' [6]He said to her, 'Because I spoke
to Naboth the Jezreelite and said to him, "Give me your vineyard
for money; or else, if you prefer, I will give you another vineyard
for it"; but he answered, "I will not give you my vineyard." ' [7]His
wife Jezebel said to him, 'Do you now govern Israel? Get up, eat
some food, and be cheerful; I will give you the vineyard of
Naboth the Jezreelite.'
[8]So she wrote letters in Ahab's name and sealed them with his
seal; she sent the letters to the elders and the nobles who lived
with Naboth in his city. [9]She wrote in the letters, 'Proclaim a fast,
and seat Naboth at the head of the assembly; [10]seat two scoundrels opposite him, and have them bring a charge against him,
saying, "You have cursed God and the king." Then take him out,
and stone him to death.' [11]The men of his city, the elders and
nobles who lived in his city, did as Jezebel had sent word to
them. Just as it was written in the letters that she had sent to
them, [12]they proclaimed a fast and seated Naboth at the head of
the assembly. [13]The two scoundrels came in and sat opposite
him; and the scoundrels brought a charge against Naboth, in the
presence of the people, saying, 'Naboth cursed God and the
king.' So they took him outside the city, and stoned him to
death. [14]Then they sent to Jezebel, saying, 'Naboth has been
stoned; he is dead.'
[15]As soon as Jezebel heard that Naboth had been stoned and was
dead, Jezebel said to Ahab, 'Go, take possession of the vineyard
of Naboth the Jezreelite, which he refused to give you for
money; for Naboth is not alive, but dead.' [16]As soon as Ahab
heard that Naboth was dead, Ahab set out to go down to the
vineyard of Naboth the Jezreelite, to take possession of it.

[17]Then the word of the Lord came to Elijah the Tishbite, saying:
[18]Go down to meet King Ahab of Israel, who rules in Samaria; he
is now in the vineyard of Naboth, where he has gone to take
possession. [19]You shall say to him, 'Thus says the Lord: Have you
killed, and also taken possession?' You shall say to him, 'Thus
says the Lord: In the place where dogs licked up the blood of
Naboth, dogs will also lick up your blood.'
[20]Ahab said to Elijah, 'Have you found me, O my enemy?' He
answered, 'I have found you. Because you have sold yourself to
do what is evil in the sight of the Lord, [21]I will bring disaster on
you; I will consume you, and will cut off from Ahab every male,
bond or free, in Israel; [22]and I will make your house like the
house of Jeroboam son of Nebat, and like the house of Baasha
son of Ahijah, because you have provoked me to anger and have
caused Israel to sin. [23]Also concerning Jezebel the Lord said, "The
dogs shall eat Jezebel within the bounds of Jezreel." [24]Anyone
belonging to Ahab who dies in the city the dogs shall eat; and
anyone of his who dies in the open country the birds of the air
shall eat.'
[25](Indeed, there was no one like Ahab, who sold himself to do
what was evil in the sight of the Lord, urged on by his wife
Jezebel. [26]He acted most abominably in going after idols, as the
Amorites had done, whom the Lord drove out before the
Israelites.)
[27]When Ahab heard those words, he tore his clothes and put
sackcloth over his bare flesh; he fasted, lay in the sackcloth, and
went about dejectedly. [28]Then the word of the Lord came to
Elijah the Tishbite: [29]'Have you seen how Ahab has humbled
himself before me? Because he has humbled himself before me, I
will not bring the disaster in his days; but in his son's days I will
bring the disaster on his house.'

Commentary

The chapter falls neatly into two parts. Verses 1-16 give an account of the corruption of the Israelite monarchy and of Israelite society, as demonstrated in the judicial murder of an innocent citizen and the seizure of his property. Verses 17-29 describe the divine response to these events through the prophetic intervention of Elijah. The episode of Naboth's vineyard is told in such a way as to highlight the cruelty of Ahab, and still more of his wife Jezebel, who are judged very severely by the deuteronomic historian (25-6). However, the narrative makes it clear that the problem extends beyond the court: without apparent effort, Jezebel is able to suborn the traditional legal system of Israel to her nefarious plot, demonstrating thereby the degree of corruption among the people at large. Lying behind this, there can be discerned a spiritual struggle between two quite different ways of understanding divine power in society. For Jezebel, the gods can be counted on to give support to the monarchy, however autocratic or self-interested its exercise of power may be. By contrast, for the editor, the prophet, and apparently also Naboth himself, royal or any other authority is always subject to the will of God set forth in *tōrah*, and must be challenged when it exceeds these bounds.

Given this starkly confrontational setting, the actual theological dynamic of prophetic intervention when it does come is surprisingly subtle and complex. There are three actors in the second half of this chapter – God, Elijah and Ahab – and each of them sees their part develop in interaction with the others. Having been summoned by God, Elijah delivers a message to Ahab which is significantly different from what he has been told (19,21-4). Having heard Elijah, Ahab is plunged into a spiritual crisis which issues in at least a partial repentance (27). Having seen Ahab's reaction, God informs Elijah that he will defer to another generation the punishment planned (29). It may well be that some of this complexity arises from the need to reconcile prophetic prediction with the subsequent course of events. Still, the scripture as it stands leads the reader deep into the relationship of God, his prophet and his people, a relationship in which justice seems to struggle with forgiveness. The apparent resolution offered by the text to this struggle raises problems both of ethical integrity and of consistency with other parts of scripture. It is best to read these verses as part of a continuing and deepening attempt within the Bible to understand the meaning of the divine attitude to Israel – an attempt within which the prophetic dialogue with God plays a crucial role.

3. The alienation of ancestral land was contrary to *tōrah*.[19] Naboth's robust response to Ahab sees the land in terms of a trust passed on to him, rather than a commodity to be traded. The royal ideology is thus at the outset signalled as being contrary to the divine plan for Israel.

4. The phrase 'resentful and sullen' repeats a description of Ahab a few verses earlier.[20] There too Ahab's sulkiness followed a rebuke for failing to keep God's law, though on that occasion his transgression was the humanitarian act of sparing the life of his enemy Ben-hadad.

5. Jezebel was for the deuteronomic historian a wholly pernicious influence, and the notoriety of her name lived on into the New Testament to refer to a figure alluring the faithful away from the purity of true belief.[21] The negative images associated with foreign wives in the Hebrew scriptures are deeply

troubling for modern readers, and it is hard to avoid a sense of xenophobia. Theologically speaking, though, anxieties were aroused by the assumption that foreigners, particularly those in powerful positions like Jezebel, would be introducing pagan cultic practices into Israel's faith. It should also be remembered that the book of Ruth provides a balance in its very positive account of the foreign-born wife of an Israelite.

7. The irritation evident in Jezebel's response expresses her highly autocratic view of kingship, presumably inherited from her own royal Sidonian upbringing.

8-14. The ease with which Jezebel's plan is carried out shows the deeply corrupt nature of Israelite society, affecting even those sectors of it ('the elders') who were particularly responsible for holding before the people the demands of social justice.

10. The charge against Naboth is the double capital crime of treason and blasphemy. According to Deuteronomy 19.15ff., those who brought false witness should themselves be subject to the punishment they had intended for the defendant. Jezebel will herself later be put to death.

13b. Naboth is led 'outside the city' – a common place of execution, but for Christian readers particularly poignant in the case of an innocent victim since it points forwards to the crucifixion of Jesus 'outside the city gate'.[22]

15. That Ahab can immediately take possession of the vineyard once Naboth is dead may mean that the property of traitors was forfeit to the crown, or it may imply that Naboth had no heirs to succeed him. If the latter is the case, then the subsequent prophetic intervention can be understood as God taking the place of Naboth's heirs in avenging his death.

19,21-4. There are several respects in which God's words to Elijah do not agree at all closely with Elijah's words to Ahab: the latter are roughly three times as long as the former; they include reference to Jezebel but omit the specific link with Naboth's fate; they are extended to cover Ahab's house and equate its doom with that of an earlier Israelite dynasty. These changes can be explained editorially as a result of the deuteronomic historian's wish to make connections between this episode and the broader narrative of the kingdom's history, and also by the need to harmonize the predictions with the actual fate of Ahab's family. Within the text as it reads now, though, they have the effect of giving Elijah a remarkable degree of prophetic licence in the transmission of the message from God to Ahab.

19. Ahab's son Joram was thrown onto Naboth's plot in explicit fulfilment of this prophecy.[23]

21,24. These verses correspond exactly to oracles delivered against Ahab's predecessor Jeroboam,[24] and are probably an editorial interpolation.

23. This additional prophecy against Jezebel is later fulfilled in gruesome literality by Jehu.[25]

25-6. The deuteronomic editor adds his wholly negative summary evaluation of Ahab.

29. The theme of God's changing his mind in response to repentance runs through Hebrew prophetic literature.[26] In this case, the adjustments involved are problematic both factually and ethically. Historically, Ahab does not at all avoid disaster; on the contrary, he dies in battle and his corpse is treated

ignominiously.[27] More troubling are the moral questions raised by God's proposal to transfer the disaster onto the next generation in his place; these cannot be wholly avoided by pointing out that Ahab's sons were in any case wicked and deserving of punishment themselves.[28] It should also be noted that a text like this stands in contradiction with the limitation of culpability to individuals proclaimed by the later prophets (Ezekiel 18).

*al-Shuʿarā*ʾ 26.123-91

The sūra *al-Shuʿarā*ʾ dates from the Makkan period. As its title implies, it takes up the contention of Muhammad's audience that the Qur'ān is the composition of 'poets' (*shuʿarā*ʾ), and thus a deliberate falsification.[29] Against this claim, the Qur'ān validates its authenticity by describing seven earlier prophets who were also dismissed as 'liars' by their contemporaries. The first two mentioned are Moses and Abraham; then follows a unified sequence of five summary narratives, each following the same pattern, telling of Noah and the four described here: Hūd, Ṣāliḥ, Lot (*Lūṭ*) and Shuʿayb. Through the sūra, the emphasis is on the integrity of the divine message and its messengers, the hostility of the rebellious societies to which it is addressed, and the consequence of catastrophic destruction as punishment for this hostility.

Qur'ānic text

123The people of ʿĀd, too, called the messengers liars. 124Their
brother Hūd said to them, 'Will you not be mindful of God? 125I
am a faithful messenger sent to you: 126be mindful of God and
obey me. 127I ask no reward of you, for my only reward is with
the Lord of the Worlds. 128How can you be so vain that you set up
monuments on every high place? 129Do you build fortresses
because you hope to be immortal? 130Why do you act like tyrants
whenever you attack someone? 131Be mindful of God and obey
me; 132be mindful of Him who has provided you with everything
you know – 133He has given you livestock, sons, 134gardens,
springs – 135for I truly fear that the torment of a grievous day will
overtake you.' 136They replied, 'It makes no difference to us
whether you warn us or not, 137for we only do what our fore-
fathers used to do: 138we shall not be punished.' 139They
denounced him as a liar, and so We destroyed them. There truly
is a sign in this, though most of them do not believe: 140your
Lord alone is the Almighty, the Merciful.

141The people of Thamūd, too, called the messengers liars.
142Their brother Ṣāliḥ said to them, 'Will you not be mindful of
God? 143I am a faithful messenger to you: 144be mindful of God

and obey me. [145]I ask no reward from you, for my only reward is with the Lord of the Worlds. [146][Do you think] you will be left secure for ever in what you have here – [147]gardens, springs, [148]fields, palm trees laden with fruit – [149]carving your fine houses from the mountains? [150]Be mindful of God and obey me: [151]do not obey those who are given to excess [152]and who spread corruption in the land instead of doing what is right.' [153]They said, 'You are bewitched! [154]You are nothing but a man like us. Show us a sign, if you are telling the truth.' [155]He said, 'Here is a camel. She should have her turn to drink and so should you, each on a specified day, [156]so do not harm her, or the punishment of a terrible day will befall you.' [157]But they hamstrung her. In the morning they had cause to regret it: [158]the punishment fell upon them. There truly is a sign in this, though most of them will not believe: [159]your Lord alone is the Almighty, the Merciful.

[160]The people of Lot, too, called the messengers liars. [161]Their brother Lot said to them, 'Will you not be mindful of God? [162]I am a faithful messenger to you: [163]be mindful of God and obey me. [164]I ask no reward from you, for my only reward is with the Lord of the Worlds. [165]Must you, unlike [other] people, lust after males [166]and abandon the wives that God has created for you? You are exceeding all bounds,' [167]but they replied, 'Lot! If you do not stop this, you will be driven away.' [168]So he said, 'I loathe what you do: [169]Lord, save me and my family from what they are doing.' [170]We saved him and all his family, [171]except for an old woman who stayed behind, [172]then We destroyed the others, [173]and poured a rain of destruction down upon them – how dreadful that rain was for those who had been forewarned. [174]There is truly a sign in this, though most of them will not believe: [175]your Lord alone is the Almighty, the Merciful.

[176]The forest-dwellers, too, called the messengers liars. [177]Shu'ayb said to them, 'Will you not be mindful of God? [178]I am a faithful messenger to you: [179]be mindful of God and obey me. [180]I ask no reward of you, for my only reward is with the Lord of the Worlds. [181]Give full measure: do not sell others short. [182]Weigh with correct scales: [183]do not deprive people of what is theirs. Do not spread corruption on earth. [184]Be mindful of God who created you and former generations,' [185]but they replied, 'You are bewitched! [186]You are nothing but a man like us. In fact we think you are a liar. [187]Make bits of the heavens fall down on us, if you are telling the truth.' [188]He said, 'My Lord knows best what you

do.' 189They called him a liar, and so the punishment of the Day
of Shadow came upon them – it was a terrible day. 190There truly
is a sign in this, though most of them will not believe: 191your
Lord alone is the Almighty, the Merciful.

Commentary

Each of the four units presented in this passage[30] follows exactly the same pattern. Using a repeated formula of stylized appeal, a prophet engages with his people, seeking to convince them of his personal integrity and of the urgency of his message, in response respectively to their accusations of lying and to their complacent persistence in unrighteousness. He is unsuccessful in this venture, however, because of the deeply rooted nature of the corruption which has gripped entire societies; as an inevitable consequence, divine punishment follows in the very radical form of the destruction of the group of people in question. The sūra thus presents together the two key Islamic themes of *taqwā*, righteous conduct carried out in consciousness of God's presence, and *ṭāʿa*, obedience to God and to his prophetic messengers. The text makes clear that the latter is closely bound up with the question of trust: the prophet first tries to persuade his people to recognize his faithfulness and then asks them to obey him. However, such is the degree of suspicion among the prophets' audiences that neither the trust nor the obedience is forthcoming; consequently, there continues also to be a failure to manifest righteous conduct.

The righteousness which the prophets enjoin has in Qur'ānic understanding a communal as well as an individual dimension;[31] correspondingly, its absence comes to characterize entire societies also. The various manifestations of wickedness have different emphases in the four societies described here as loci of prophetic activity, but it is possible to discern within the teachings addressed to the various groups of people a common set of divinely authorized values which form the core of Islamic ethics. In this way – as the commonalty of form between the different units makes clear – it is neither desirable nor possible in Islamic terms to make distinctions between the various prophets, who all deliver the same basic message. Moreover, they are in this sūra all authenticated by God in the same way, namely the enactment of punitive consequences on disbelieving societies. Clearly there are some ethical issues raised in connection with these accounts: even within contexts as corrupt as those described here, there may be some individuals striving to live righteous lives, and it seems unjust that they should suffer the fate of others. This is already recognized to some extent in the way in which the prophets themselves (and for Lot, his family also) are delivered from the calamities which befall others. In Muhammad's time, the separation out of the righteous from a corrupt society was to achieve normative form in the *ḥijra* of Muslims from a minority status in Makka to the Madinan setting where they were free to practise a fully Islamic way of life.

123-4,141-2. The peoples of ʿĀd and Thamūd are generally considered to be Arab groups, and the prophets Hūd and Ṣāliḥ – neither of whom corresponds to a biblical figure[32] – are seen as Arabic-speaking prophets in the period between Noah and Abraham.

123-7. Each prophet's message begins by engaging his auditors in exactly the same words. This uniformity of style is an exemplification of the principle of 'making no distinction between all the prophets'.[33]

124. As with all the prophets in this sequence, Hūd's identification with the people of the society to which he is sent is emphasized by describing him as 'their brother'.

128-9. ʿĀd is pictured as a powerful and sophisticated civilization. The Qur'ān elsewhere[34] describes its people as being of exceptional stature.

132-3. The sin of unbelief according to the Qur'ān is *kufr*, connoting 'ingratitude': the people of ʿĀd culpably fail to acknowledge God as the source of the blessings they enjoy.

137. ʿĀd displays unreasoning attachment to idolatrous traditions inherited from the past, and is not prepared to make the radical break with a corrupt past required by genuine monotheism.

139a. Elsewhere, the Qur'ān explains that the destruction of ʿĀd was effected by a ferocious wind,[35] and that God saved his prophet Hūd from the calamity.[36]

139b-140. Each of the four units of text describing a prophet ends with the same words. A 'sign' (*āya*) is a demonstration of truth which is naturally evident, though its meaning will not be discerned in a corrupt society.

141-2. See above on 123-4.

146-52. Thamūd's complacent self-sufficiency and its love of luxury blind its people to an awareness of their dependence and mortality, and engender excess and corruption.

155. The commentators generally interpret this sign by explaining that the camel would drink water one day and the citizens of Thamūd on another; on the day that the camel drank, the people would drink her milk. The primary point of the sign is thus that it shows a rationally ordered, self-restrained system of symbiosis. For some commentators, a more obviously supernatural element is added by the story that the camel is brought into being miraculously.

157. The corruption of Thamūd's society is such that the model system of human and camel sharing resources is wilfully destroyed by an act of cruel vandalism.

158. This verse speaks in unspecific terms of 'the punishment'; in other places, the Qur'ān refers to the punitive destruction of Thamūd through an 'earthquake', 'scream' or 'bolt'.[37]

165. The people of Lot are reproached for the sin of homosexual lust, as likewise Sodom in Genesis 18. The means of destruction also corresponds to that in the biblical account.

171. Commentators explain that the woman destroyed was Lot's wife (as in Genesis 19.26).

176-7. In other passages of the Qur'ān, Shu'ayb is described as being sent to Midian. It is a disputed point in the commentarial tradition as to whether the 'forest' should be identified with Midian.[38] There is also debate over the identification of Shu'ayb with the biblical figure of Jethro, priest of Midian and father-in-law of Moses.[39]

181-3. The prophetic message in this context is one of fair dealing in trade, a theme recurrent in the Hebrew scriptures also.[40]

187. The people of the forest seek to test the prophet by asking him himself to be the one who enacts the divine punishment – in response to which he clearly enunciates the limits of prophetic responsibility set against the power of God.[41]

Questions from the scriptures

The texts which describe prophetic interventions in society are all written from a later viewpoint, which can look back on a time of disputation assured of the authenticity of the message brought by the prophet, and thus clear in its perceptions of the alternatives of acceptance or rejection. The scriptures themselves reflect this *post eventum* stance, and interpret an earlier generation's reactions to prophecy with the assurance of hindsight. Yet such clarity of perspective may not have been available to all or even most in the actual time and place of the prophet's mission. Jezebel may indeed have consciously been working evil, but Ahab's course of action was much more messily ambiguous; the people of Noah's time had no rational reason for believing in the disaster he predicted. How were these people to discern the truth of prophecy in their own time?

Similar questions arise for us in our own situation. How are we to know prophetic religion in the world today? At a time when extremist and hateful attitudes and actions are justified in the name of religion, how are we to distinguish a genuinely prophetic word from a message of hatred or violence? How can we tell the difference between the divisions and ruptures which are truly necessitated by the divine Word and those which are the result of human sin and divisiveness? In situations where social bonds are fragile, is it possible to conceive of genuine prophecy as that which further divides people?

On the other hand, the divine Word requires justice, and this cannot be simply traded for a superficial peace. Where does prophetic religion impel Christians and Muslims today to speak and act against an unjust society? Are there ways in which we can speak and act together? What kind of reception can we expect from our contemporaries?

These are questions about the discernment of prophetic responsibility in a world where clear prophetic guidance is not directly or evidently available. That brings us back to the searching and interpretation of our scriptures, reading them in the light of our time and place and reading our time and place in the light of the scriptures, and asking 'Where is the Word of God to be found in this?'

Chapter 5

Jesus and Muhammad

The centrality of Jesus to Christians, and of Muhammad to Muslims, is obvious. Within each religion, rich devotional and theological traditions have been developed to express an understanding of who Jesus is for Christians, and who Muhammad is for Muslims. The terms which those two traditions use differ greatly from one another – not least in the importance of the category of 'prophet'. The two essays presented here seek to cross-reference these separate discourses by appraising and interrogating each other's tradition from the viewpoint of the other faith. Thus, Mahmoud Ayoub offers a Muslim's response to the Christian understanding of Jesus, while Dan Madigan responds as a Christian to the Muslim view of Muhammad.

'Īsā and Jesus: Christ in Islamic Christology

Mahmoud Ayoub

Who is the Muslim *'Īsā* in relation to Jesus Christ as Christians understand him?[1] To answer this question fully would involve an examination of the full range of Christology as that has developed within the Christian Churches, but here I will restrict myself to the trajectories of the New Testament only.

It must be remembered that Islam was born into a Christian milieu – that is to say, into an environment which was permeated by Christian piety as well as by Jewish monotheism. I am convinced that it was to this Christian tradition that the Prophet referred when he declared: 'I sense the breath of the All-merciful (*nafas al-raḥman*) from the Yemen',[2] for the Christianity which the Qur'ān knows is not that of either Byzantium or Rome. Rather, it is the devotion of desert monks and other pious men and women, living as hermits and in small communities in the Arabian desert. For these Christians, Christ was in the first place a saviour, a conqueror of demonic powers, a bringer of holiness. The Islamic Christology which grows out of this context, attested as it is by the Qur'ān and by the prophetic tradition, needs to be taken seriously, and considered on its own merits, as a witness to the fuller understanding of who Jesus is for humanity.

In the Gospel of John, Jesus is pre-eminently the divine *Logos*. As such, he is the agent of creation and the Word of truth, become incarnate in, involved in, human life. The Qur'ān also calls Jesus *kalimat Allāh*, the 'Word of God',[3] cast into Mary by God. This does not imply that the *Logos* is the Second Person of the Trinity. Rather, it means that Christ came into being, not through the usual processes of cause and effect, but by the direct command and as the direct creation of God – 'Let there be Christ,' said God, 'and there was Christ'. Islam thus distinguishes clearly between recognizing Jesus as the Word of God, on the one hand, and claiming that Jesus is God, on the other hand. It is the latter that is a problematic issue between Muslims and Christians.[4] The Qur'ān also calls Jesus a 'spirit from God'.[5] Later Muslim tradition was to use the more absolute form 'Spirit of God',[6] but this too clearly has a different import to the use of 'Spirit' in the Christian theology of the Trinity. It is undoubtedly the case that the idea of Jesus as 'Word of God' has not been adequately studied by Muslims. This is in contrast to the great amount of thought which has been devoted to the theology of the Qur'ān as the Word of God, and this obvious parallel raises a corresponding question to that about the Qur'ān which has generated so much controversy within Islam: 'Is Jesus as Word of God created or uncreated?' It may be that the answer we have to give is along the lines of 'neither this nor yet that'.

The Qur'ānic account of the birth of Jesus is not unlike the annunciation narrative to be found in the Gospel of Luke.[7] The Qur'ān indeed depicts the relationship between Jesus and God in terms of familiarity and closeness. For this reason, most Islamic commentators have no real problem in describing Jesus as a 'son of God', provided this is interpreted in a metaphorical way, and is not taken to imply an actual identity between Jesus and God, or to implicate God in anything resembling an act of physical generation.[8]

The Qur'ān also speaks of the miracles of Jesus. The emphasis here is consistently on the life-giving power which they display – for example, the raising of the dead, or the breathing of life into birds made of clay.[9] These are signs of the glory of God, performed by the permission of God, rather than independently enacted pointers to Jesus' own glory. They point to the character of the Word of God which takes shape in Jesus as being itself a miracle of life, a vivifying and sanctifying divine force which cannot be restricted to the one event of his earthly life, but continues for ever as a source of life, blessing and guidance for humanity.[10]

The claims to Messianic status made for Jesus, by himself and by others, can be taken seriously by Muslims, and appear to be endorsed by the Qur'ān.[11] What is unusual about Jesus' understanding of this role is that it teaches the suffering of the Messiah – an insight which is particularly congenial to the Shi'ite tradition. At the same time, the Qur'ān also affirms that Jesus as Messiah will eventually triumph over the forces of evil, personified in Muslim tradition by the figure of the anti-Christ, *al-Dajjāl*. In some sense, Jesus can thus be seen by Muslims as a source of salvation, inasmuch as guidance to healing is taken to be the way by which God saves humanity.

Other New Testament passages which can be aligned with an Islamic Christology include Acts 2–4 and Hebrews 1.1-4.[12] In the former, Christology is expressed primarily in the categories of Jewish Messianism; there is a sense in which the Lukan Christ does not appear to be completely divine, but rather to be defined by his functional relationship to God, and this makes it possible to see Islamic Christology as a continuation of this tradition, sustained among Jewish and Eastern Christians. When we speak of the Word in relation to God, we are not daring to say anything about the inner essence of the divine, but to refer to the outward expression of the divine towards us.

In the passage from Hebrews, I believe that we should take very seriously the language of 'the fullness of time', for it opens up the possibility of a recognition that God may truly have spoken, and truly speak still, through both the Christ and the Qur'ān. It is within a radically inclusive or plural framework of this kind that we need to conduct dialogue in a spirit of respect and equality. The different religions of humanity do not have to be cast as rivals or even enemies. If God is loving and merciful, we need to be open to all the ways in which he may be speaking through different divinely chosen channels to our different contexts. Christians and Muslims must abandon their exclusivist claims to one another and to others, and treat with one another on a basis of equality and mutual recognition. This is in reality the position adopted by the Qur'ān itself, though often denied in the later, and current, interpretations of Muslim scholars.[13]

One of the most difficult issues between Christians and Muslims has been the Gospel accounts of the death by crucifixion of Jesus, and the Qur'ān's apparent denials of this.[14] Yet the Qur'ān is not ultimately interested in the question of whether or not Jesus was crucified, and it does speak elsewhere in clear terms of Jesus dying at some point in time.[15] The comment regarding those who thought they had crucified Jesus that 'so it seemed to them'[16] is not intended to portray a divine deception of any kind, but to cancel out the thought that anybody could put an end to all that Jesus did: as the life-giving Word from God, he could not be silenced.

If we can learn to engage seriously and respectfully with one another in the ways I have tried to outline in this area of Christology, then we can move into a dialogue wherein neither condescends to the other, but we address one another on a basis of equality as fellow seekers of the divine will. Then we can start building, not merely bridges towards one another, but a highway towards the one God.

Jesus and Muhammad: The sufficiency of prophecy

Daniel Madigan

The question of Muhammad is without doubt the most avoided question in Muslim–Christian relations. One finds no mention of the Prophet of Islam, for example, in the otherwise laudatory comments made about Muslims and their faith in the groundbreaking documents of the Second Vatican Council. They give no sense at all that this faith has a founder and a history. And since that time the hesitancy about responding could hardly be said to have diminished.

The question posed is carefully worded, or at least it shows all the marks of being so. I am asked to give a Christian response to the Muslim understanding of Muhammad. There are two extremely important elements in that formulation: first of all it is to be a response to *the Muslim understanding of* Muhammad – as distinct from a response to Muhammad. Secondly, of all the kinds of response it might be, it is to be a Christian response.

It is not possible simply to give a response to Muhammad, since anyone not belonging to the generation of his Companions has to rely on the witness of the believing community to know something of him. What one responds to, whether believer or not, is the *image* of the Prophet proposed by the community for whom half the creed is '*Muḥammad rasūl Allāh*' – Muhammad is God's messenger. We do not have any other sources on which to rely – or at least nothing that could claim more authority, or objectivity, or historical proximity. Even polemical works directed against Muhammad are not based on first-hand experience of him, or on independent historical sources. They are, rather, responses to the image of Muhammad proposed by the Muslim community.

So in order to respond, I have to ask 'which Muhammad' or which *image* of Muhammad are we talking about? Very often one responds to the image of the Prophet offered by the standard biography of Ibn Isḥāq, composed from traditional materials about a hundred years after Muhammad's death. The *Sīra*, as it is called, was an extraordinarily detailed account not only of the career of the Prophet but also of the history of his family and tribe, indeed of the history of prophecy itself. We have only an edited version of it dating from the ninth century, and citations from it in other works. In one way or another all biographies of Muhammad are based upon it. We have looked together at a passage from it recounting Muhammad's first encounter with the revelation.

One of the things that most strikes the Christian reader of the *Sīra* is the concentration on Muhammad's military campaigns, his strategy of creating a power base from which to consolidate the new religion, along with the inexorable expansion of his authority and military dominance. Muhammad in this respect was no Jesus. However, this element of the *Sīra* (called *maghāzī* literature) is not unlike the military material we are familiar with from the Old Testament – God dictates goals and strategy, and grants victory to the believers as long as they act according to the divine will.

An early recorded response to the question of Muhammad is that of the Nestorian Patriarch Timothy I in his eighth-century dialogue with the third ʿAbbasid Caliph, al-Mahdī (d. 785).[17] I doubt that in the twelve centuries since that conversation (much elaborated in subsequent literary versions) we have progressed much beyond the Patriarch's response. He chooses his words carefully: 'It is clear', he says, 'that Muhammad walked in the path of the prophets.' He mentions Muhammad's preaching of monotheism, his strictures against idolatry and polytheism, his institution of authentic worship, and his ethical teaching and leadership, all evidence that Muhammad 'walked in the path of the prophets'. Citing particularly the example of Moses, who slew the Israelites who had worshipped the Golden Calf,[18] Timothy praises Muhammad's willingness to commit himself to the cause of God not only in word but also in action, with force of arms, and he takes that as one of the proofs of Muhammad's having 'walked in the path of the prophets'.[19] He cites only this one example, but he could have chosen any number of such instances of divinely sanctioned violence from the career of Moses or other biblical prophets – sometimes the slaughter is the punishment for unbelief, but in other cases it is merely because the victims stand between the people of Israel and the land of the promise.

Timothy was hardly scandalized by the power exercised by Muhammad in the service of God's message and of the community that formed around it. He interprets the success of the Muslims against the Persian and Byzantine empires as the just punishment of God for the idolatry of the former and the heresy of the latter – remember we are dealing with a Nestorian patriarch. Prophecy, according to the Old Testament model to which he appeals, is expected to use all means at its disposal in the service of truth. The sovereignty of God has always somehow to be translated into this-worldly terms, and no one is surprised if that sovereignty seems to command combat or even slaughter. This is not an exclusively Islamic or Jewish attitude and it has a prominent place in the history of the Christian Churches as well, even if not in the life of Jesus or the early period of his community. Timothy has the insight and honesty to recognize that the question of religion and power is one that faces us all. He does not pretend that Christians have traditionally resolved it differently from Muslims or Jews. A conviction about the ultimate truth which hesitates to assert that truth and to put it into practice is arguably no conviction at all.

Two things should be noted about Timothy's response. The first is what might seem a certain evasiveness in his formulation. After saying that Muhammad had done everything the other prophets did, why not just say that he too was a prophet? A major reason for this, though Timothy may have had others, is that to say 'Muhammad is a prophet' is in effect to pronounce the second part of the *shahāda*, the Muslim profession of faith. Since Christians already profess belief in one God, affirming the prophethood of Muhammad could be said to complete the process of declaring oneself a Muslim. The Christian cannot share the fullness of Muslim faith that this man is the bearer of the ultimate divine Word to humanity, and further that he is the definitive interpreter of that Word, and the model for a human life lived in faithful response to the Word and will of God. But having said that, we are not reduced to silence. We still have a duty to respond.

Muslims often complain that Christians will not reciprocate their acknowledgement of Jesus as a prophet by recognizing the prophethood of Muhammad. Yet such a recognition would not constitute a real act of reciprocity, for Muslims acknowledge about Jesus only what the Qur'ān says of him, not what Christians say of him. True reciprocation would involve Muslim acceptance of Christian faith about Jesus in return for a Christian acknowledgement of Muhammad. Timothy goes probably as far as a Christian can go, and certainly much further than most Christians are prepared to go, in the estimation of Muhammad.

The second thing about Timothy's response is its fundamentally positive approach. We may think it rather politic, given that he was answering a caliph in whose hands rested his own fate and that of his community. However, as Bishop Kenneth Cragg pointed out about twenty years ago, our response to the question of Muhammad is not simply a matter of revisiting past doctrinal conflicts. It is a question of working actively to develop understandings that might take us towards a more creative future.[20] Timothy's positive response to the Caliph opened a way forward in the eighth century. However, that path by and large was not and still is not taken.

Timothy's response showed us what a Christian response should be: collaborative rather than competitive, seeking out and welcoming the undoubted resonances in the diverse Muslim images of Muhammad, and the familiar echoes in the Qur'ān of a revelation already heard. These resonances are often dismissed as indications of dependence, borrowing or imitation. However, it is also possible to see in them a confirmation of our shared attentiveness to the God who continually seeks to address us 'in many and varied ways' as the writer of the letter to the Hebrews puts it. Before there is any prophecy or scripture, there is the divine Word, which in both our traditions is considered pre-eternal.

This, I think, is crucial. Behind a Muslim's question about Muhammad lies, I believe, another more personal, perhaps more urgent, question: 'Do you take me seriously as someone attentive to the Word of God?' 'Do you respect me as someone listening sincerely for what God has to say and ready to act on it?' Professor Ayoub has said in discussion that in the final analysis the Christian's response to the question of Muhammad does not matter. He does not feel the need for Christian approval of his faith in Muhammad as God's messenger. And he does not want a grudging response, so conditioned and circumscribed that it becomes virtually meaningless. The question about attentiveness to the Word of God, on the other hand, seems to me to matter enormously, because it is a question about the bona fides of the other.

Can Christians take Muhammad seriously as someone who listened for the Word of God? Indeed I think we can – the Muhammad we know through Muslim proclamation of him is, for the reasons the Patriarch Timothy outlined, a serious listener for the Word. As the first Companions heard from him the word that he had heard, so the Muslim community listens together with him for the Word – listening not just *to* the Qur'ān but *through* the Qur'ān, opening themselves to the infinite power of God's Word to signify anew in each historical situation. Our way forward, perhaps our only way forward, is on the basis of our recognition of one another as sincere listeners for the Word.

Having said all this about Timothy's response to the classical *Sīra* image of Muhammad, it has to be noted that, when Muslims speak of the Prophet, one finds that it is rarely simply the Prophet presented in the *Sīra*. The portraits they propose either concentrate on one or other aspect of that *Sīra* image, or are developed from the variety of sayings and actions attributed to the Prophet. Sometimes they go well beyond either *Sīra* or *Sunna*, straying even beyond the consensus of orthodoxy in their speculations. The image of Muhammad any particular Muslim has in mind when affirming that he is *rasūl Allāh* will draw on many sources and reflect various ideals, not all of them compatible:

Muhammad the fiery prophet defending the rights of the poor and denouncing the godless arrogance of the powerful. The religious and social reformer, patient and constant under persecution and rejection. Muhammad the faithful monotheist when virtually all about him were idolaters. Muhammad the charismatic preacher who listened intently for the Word of God, who preached what he heard and practised to perfection what he preached. Muhammad the sometimes harsh, sometimes merciful, ever astute statesman and military commander. The bearer of definitive truth that relativizes and corrects all other beliefs. The founder of an Arab tribal confederation that within a short space of time dominated half the known world. Muhammad the affectionate father, the gentle and witty husband who could laugh at the intrigues and jealousies of his household. The worker of signs and wonders who split the moon, to whom trees bowed, and whose touch healed and brought forth abundance. Muhammad the wise judge and model of perfection, to be followed in the minutest details of behaviour. Muhammad the rationalist reformer and proponent of a modern civilization *avant le mot*. The consummate philosopher who nonetheless clothed truth in the garb of religion in order to accommodate himself to the masses. Muhammad, the beautiful, the tenderly beloved of God and the mystic's bridegroom. Muhammad, the primordial light through which everything is created. Muhammad who penetrated the highest heaven and was admitted to the very presence of God. Muhammad, sent by God 'as a mercy for the ages', the sole intercessor before God whose prayer will be heard and upon whom, therefore, salvation depends.[21]

Ultimately the Christian hesitancy about responding positively to images of Muhammad has been the sense that any response is always at least an implied comparison with Jesus. I would like to say two things about this. The first is that it is a confusion of categories. Though Jesus may be thought of in Islamic tradition as being in the same category as Muhammad, the Christian does not see things in this way. Jesus for the Christian is not just a different style of prophet, or a better class of prophet. For Christians Jesus is not the bearer of the Word of God in the way Muhammad is for Muslims. Rather he is that Word, the embodiment of that Word – the 'incarnation', we say, the enfleshment of the Word. As in Muslim understanding God chose 'clear Arabic language' to communicate the Word in the Qur'ān, so in the Christian understanding God chose what we might call body-language – the language of embodied human living, and dying – to express the Word in Jesus.

Muslim faith does not claim that Muhammad is the Word, but rather that he is the human channel through whom the Word entered the world – an Arab prophet to give voice to the Word of God addressed to the Arabs in their own language. In this respect he is like Mary in the Christian scheme of things – the human person whose cooperation was needed to give flesh to the Word. As Seyyed Hossein Nasr pointed out, just as the Christian doctrine of Mary's virginity expresses the conviction that what comes from her is from God, so the doctrine of Muhammad's illiteracy plays a similar role in the Muslim understanding of revelation.[22]

By his words and example Muhammad is understood to be the definitive interpreter of the Word. His preaching creates a new community and leads it out of persecution, establishing a new identity and a new polity. He gives political expression to the truth of faith. As interpreter he is like Paul; as liberator and legislator he is a Moses figure – without parallel in the Christian tradition; as political and military leader his role resembles that of Constantine.

Christian responses to Muslim images of Muhammad tend to confound these categories and presume that Muhammad is being proposed as a replacement saviour. Yet that is not what Muslims generally believe of him. Similarly, Muslim responses to Christian faith in Jesus often miss the parallel with their faith in the Qur'ān. For Muslims the Qur'ān comes as a Word not to be interrogated and analysed but to be received, believed and obeyed. It speaks for itself and, even though it must be listened to in diverse situations and thus interpreted, it *must* be listened to since it claims to be a divine Word. Muslims would not consider that they have raised an otherwise human message to the level of the divine. And so they do not sense themselves free to reduce the status of the Qur'ān to one word among many. No more do most Christians understand themselves entitled to reduce the status of Jesus, whom Christian faith experiences as the divine Word. He is believed in neither as one word among many, nor as one prophet among many. Our dialogue, therefore, is not a process of negotiating claims until we reach a common denominator. Rather its purpose is to learn precisely from our differences where the uniqueness of each lies.

Is Muhammad's preaching, then, superfluous for a Christian? Not at all. On the contrary it is invaluable, since it contains a salutary critique of Christian faith and behaviour. Its refusal of what it understands as some key points of Christian faith offers us the opportunity to re-examine and refine a proclamation that had failed to convey a clear sense of its monotheistic nature; that had failed to convey the central significance of the cross; that had perhaps forgotten that its religious language of fatherhood, motherhood and sonship was figurative rather than simply literal. In a sense it could be said that we stand in need of the Qur'ān's critique in order to come to a fuller understanding of our faith. The questions raised by that critique have received answers and prompted refinements, but principally in the Eastern Christian tradition. For obvious historical and geographical reasons Western theology did not have a strong sense of a Muslim interlocutor, and so addressed other audiences, refining its thought and its theological language in conversation with classical philosophy, Enlightenment rationalism and humanist scepticism. Now, however, Western theology has a task and an opportunity before it.

The second theme running through our text studies is the question of the sufficiency of prophecy. We must first ask, 'Sufficiency for what?' For salvation? No, not exactly. Both our traditions would agree that our salvation depends on nothing but God's gracious mercy, though the preaching of prophets and apostles is surely to be considered one aspect of that mercy. We lay hold of that salvation by believing, as St Paul puts it and the Qur'ān would surely agree, in the one 'who gives life to the dead and calls into existence the things that do not exist'.[23] That for Paul is the faith of Abraham.

Professor Kadi has described (see chapter 3) how in the Qur'ānic understanding (which is only one element, albeit the most authoritative, of the Islamic understanding) prophecy is instituted by God to call us back to the primordial divine–human covenant. It is a mercy in that it makes possible a new adherence to the covenant. And it is on the basis of our faithfulness to the covenant that we will be judged. To this extent the revelation is seen as salvific, though the Qur'ān stresses that no amount of preaching to those destined to disbelieve will bring them to faith.[24]

The question remains, however, whether a word of command, reminder and guidance is adequate to deal with the human predicament. Are human beings merely forgetful, unreflective, lacking in knowledge, or is there more to our rejection of God than can be resolved by a sharp rebuke and a firm guiding hand? Although Christians recognize as well as Muslims the sovereignty of the Word of God – God's absolute right to command and our absolute duty to obey – we have also seen in human history, as well as experienced personally, the inability of a merely commanding word to transform its hearers. Our rebellion seems to run deeper than that. We have come to realize, and occasionally admit, the bitter truth that left to ourselves we are incapable of fulfilling the command of God – not because it is too demanding, but because we begrudge our obedience and feel unjustly stifled by any limits on our freedom.

Humans are born in an almost unbearable tension between being created and being creative. This tension we all experience is not an original evil, nor a flaw in our nature, but rather the inevitable result of an original gift. Of all creatures only human beings have been given a share in God's creativity; but that creativity must nonetheless be exercised within the givenness of a creation already in existence. Sin, in this case, is the refusal, in one direction or another, to live as a creative creature. It is either an attempt to live solely as creator – shaping my world as though I were the final arbiter of how it should be; refusing to recognize the limits on me that make space for the other (both human, animal and inanimate creation); refusing to observe 'how things work' in creation as it is and pretending it is different. Or else sin is an attempt to avoid the demands of creativity and live as though I were merely a creature – no more able to respond to the needs of other beings than a cow or a snail, and therefore no more responsible than they would be for failures towards others and towards creation. The art of human living is to live the tension fruitfully. There is no evil involved – God did not create us evil or prone to sin. God gave us a share in the divine creativity. It is an extraordinary gift, but hard to manage. Though the accounts of the book of Genesis dramatize for us the failure to balance these two aspects of our nature, they do not offer us an explanation of our proneness to sin, other than this awkward union of creativity and creatureliness.

Looking at our history, it seems that clearer enunciation of the sovereign word and more detailed exposition of its demands have not succeeded in dealing with human sin. Even promises and threats seem powerless to liberate us from what holds us bound. Faced with human rebelliousness God cannot simply abandon all sovereignty, and tailor his demands to our fitful obedience. Yet for God to judge us as we deserve would entail the annihilation of humanity, for none of us deserves to be saved. However, Christians have seen in Jesus another way of God's exercising sovereignty: a sovereignty of love, which does not stand on its own prerogatives; a vulnerable sovereignty; a sovereignty that pours itself out in love; a sovereign who washes the feet of his subjects; who reigns not from a throne but from a gibbet, not in a citadel but outside the city. This sovereign does not indulge our disobedience or wink at our defiance, but rather bears the brunt of it, endures the cost of it, thus ultimately robbing it of its power. Our humanity is rescued from its mortality not by being sent information and commands but by the transformation that is effected by its being assumed in love by the divine.

Prophecy, then, to the extent that it is thought of simply as warning, prompting and lawgiving, will seem to a Christian insufficient to reassure us that we have been or will be rescued from what we know of our own reality.

The question remains to what extent the Islamic tradition sees this kind of prophecy as sufficient. It is all too common to caricature Islam as a religion in which the divine remains utterly transcendent and in which the role of love is kept well under control. This is a caricature because, even if one might be able to make a case from the Qur'ān for such an idea (though certainly not a watertight case!), there are other strong and consistent strands in the *ḥadīth* and in non-canonical religious literature where we see evidence of a movement towards a belief in the intimate involvement of divinity with humanity, especially focused in the person and ministry of the Prophet. Some of these were listed earlier: the strong doctrine of intercession explicit in the *ḥadīth* even though quite circumscribed in the Qur'ān; the veneration of the Prophet and the love mysticism of the Sufi tradition; the meditation on the names of the Prophet in parallel with the divine names – and the fact that several of those names are shared by both; speculation about the cosmic significance of the Prophet as the primordial light reflecting the divine light; the idea of Muhammad as the first-born of creation for whose sake the rest of the universe was created: in a Divine Saying (*ḥadīth qudsī*) God addresses the Prophet saying, *Lawlāka, lawlāka, ma khalaqnā al-aflāk,* 'But for you, but for you, we would not have created the celestial spheres.'

In all this perhaps we are seeing evidence that, in the Islamic tradition as well, prophecy understood simply as bearing a word of guidance and command is felt to be insufficient either to express the greatness of God and the richness of God's mercy or to meet humanity's profound need for transformation.

Chapter 6

The completion of prophecy

In very different ways, both Muslims and Christians believe that prophecy reaches its completion in Muhammad and Jesus respectively. The scriptural material on these two figures is differently weighted. While Muhammad of course features centrally in the Qur'ān, he does not appear by name in the Bible, although some Muslims would see his advent as heralded by some Gospel passages. On the other hand, Jesus is not only the central actor in the drama of the New Testament, but also is the subject of many Qur'ānic passages, some of which also refer to his mother Mary. This chapter brings together texts from both scriptures concerning Jesus' conception by Mary, as well as shorter passages which speak of the endings of prophecy brought through Jesus and Muhammad.

Scripture dialogue V

Maryam 19.16-36; Luke 1.26-38

The figure of Mary (*Maryam*) is held in special esteem by both Muslims and Christians. In both faiths, she is acknowledged to be the mother of Jesus, miraculously conceiving her child as a virgin; in both also, she is seen as an exemplar of obedience and holy living. In neither can she be straightforwardly identified as a prophet, though her involvement with the event of prophetic activity is intimate. There are significantly divergent emphases in the way that Mary is portrayed in Islam and in Christianity, and some of these are clearly linked to the sharp doctrinal differences that separate Muslims and Christians over the person and work of her son Jesus.

Maryam 19.16-36

Maryam is a sūra dating from Muhammad's prophetic activity in Makka. Persecution of the Muslim community there was so harsh that a group sought refuge with the Christian king (*negus*) of Ethiopia. Asked about their faith, it was a portion of this sūra which they recited, thereby convincing the *negus* that their faith was sufficiently close to his for him to extend his protection to them. The portion discussed here follows after an account of Zachariah; the sūra subsequently goes on to mention Abraham and Moses, and then attacks the false beliefs of Muhammad's pagan contemporaries. The verses below are marked by a strong poetic rhythm, which has led some to suggest that they may reflect knowledge of Syriac liturgical material in honour of Mary. Unfortunately, our knowledge of early Christianity in Arabia is so meagre that the ways in which earlier Christian traditions may have been taken up and reshaped by the Qur'ānic revelation cannot now be clearly discerned.

Qur'ānic text

[16]Mention in the Qur'ān the story of Mary. She withdrew from
her family to a place to the east [17]and secluded herself away; We
sent Our Spirit to appear before her in the form of a perfected
man. [18]She said, 'I seek the Lord of Mercy's protection against
you: if you have any fear of Him [do not approach]!' [19]but he
said, 'I am but a Messenger from your Lord, [come] to announce
to you the gift of a pure son.' [20]She said, 'How can I have a son
when no man has touched me? I have not been unchaste,' [21]and
he said, 'This is what your Lord said: "It is easy for Me – We shall
make him a sign to all people, a blessing from Us." ' [22]And so it
was ordained: she conceived him. She withdrew to a distant
place [23]and when the pains of childbirth drove her to [cling to]
the trunk of a palm tree, she exclaimed, 'I wish I had been long
dead and forgotten before all this!' [24]but a voice cried to her from
below, 'Do not worry: your Lord has provided a stream at your
feet [25]and, if you shake the trunk of the palm tree towards you, it
will deliver fresh ripe dates for you, [26]so eat, drink, be glad, and
say to anyone you may see: "I have vowed to the Lord of Mercy
to abstain from conversation, and I will not talk to anyone
today." '

[27]She went back to her people carrying the child, and they said,
'Mary! You must have done something terrible! [28]Sister of Aaron!
Your father was not an evil man; your mother was not unchaste!'
[29]She pointed at him. They said, 'How can we converse with an
infant?' [30][But] he said: 'I am a servant of God. He has granted
me the Scripture; made me a prophet; [31]made me blessed wher-
ever I may be – He commanded me to pray, to give alms as long
as I live, [32]to cherish my mother – He did not make me domin-
eering or graceless. [33]Peace was on me the day I was born, and
will be on me the day I die and the day I am raised to life again.'
[34]Such was Jesus, son of Mary.

[This is] a statement of the Truth about which they are in doubt:

[35]it would not befit God to have a child. He is far above that: when He decrees something, He says only, 'Be,' and it is. [36]'God is my Lord and your Lord, so serve Him: that is a straight path.'

Commentary

This is the longer of two substantial Qur'ānic passages concerning Mary the mother of Jesus.[1] The focus of the main part of the narrative (16-28) is on Mary herself: stress is laid on her seclusion and chastity, and subsequently on the declaration of her innocence in the face of slanderous accusations. The underlying motif in these verses is that of the divine vindication of an outcast in the desert. Such an emphasis is of course consonant with the Qur'ān's general attitude to those entrusted by God to carry his message to humanity, and exegetes have discussed whether Mary herself should be counted as a prophet. In fact, this has remained a minority opinion;[2] most have restricted prophetic status in the formal sense to males only. Nevertheless, it is clear that Mary is the key figure in a prophetic event – her visitor is described as a 'messenger (*rasūl*)' from God, and a divinely inspired 'scripture (*kitāb*)' is to be the outcome of her son's birth. To some extent, the underlying dynamic of this narrative can be compared to the Gospel account of the annunciation, though its distinctively Islamic inflexions must also be noted. Christians in history and today have often been both surprised and heartened by the respect in which Mary is held by Muslims.

This sense of convergence, however, needs to be set against the words attributed to the newly born Jesus and the Qur'ān's own underlining of their implications (30-36). Jesus' declaration in this context serves two functions. In terms of the narrative of Mary, certainly, it dramatically vindicates her against her calumniators. At the same time, it is directed towards Muhammad's Christian contemporaries, presenting them with a concise statement of Islamic Christology and inviting them to turn away from what it sees as their errors arising from excessive devotion to Jesus and his mother.[3] It is striking indeed that one and the same Qur'ānic passage should at once bring the two communities of faith so close together and yet also delineate so sharply the reality of the difference which separates them. The earliest Christian auditor of this sūra declared that between his faith and the Muslims' there was a difference no thicker than a line[4] – yet that line has a permanent and irreducible significance of its own.

16-17a. Mary's seclusion is described as her going behind a 'veil' (*hijāb*). Some commentators suggest that this may have been for cleansing after her monthly period, i.e. that she was entering a ritual bath (the Jewish *mikveh*). Whatever detailed explanation is given, it is clear that this verse stresses Mary's isolation in purity – for some Sufi writers, this became a sign of the inward withdrawal necessary to receive spiritual guidance.

17b. 'Our Spirit' (*rūḥanā*) is generally considered by Muslim exegetes to be the angel Gabriel. In this passage, the Spirit is personified in human form; elsewhere, the Qur'ān refers to God's 'breathing' the Spirit into Mary.[5] He is in any case a 'messenger' (*rasūl*) of God.

18-20. Mary's alarm, and the messenger's reassurance, echo closely the exchange between Mary and Gabriel as told in the Gospel.[6] The theme of Mary's maintenance of her chastity is repeated in the Qur'ān.[7]

22. The parenthetic assertion that the conception of Jesus was 'ordained' is used by Ash'arite theologians as a proof text for their theory that human actions are determined in advance by the divine will. The Qur'ānic account strikingly includes no reference to a conscious act of assent by Mary.

23. The symbol of the palm tree has become common in Islamic culture, where it recalls not only Mary but also Muhammad, who leant on a palm tree while delivering his sermons.[8] The parallel between Christian veneration of Mary as bearer of Jesus the divine Word and Islamic devotion to Muhammad as bearer of the divine Word of the Qur'ān is a suggestive one.[9]

24. The identity of the 'voice from below' is not clear; it may be the angel Gabriel acting in the role of 'midwife' to Mary, or it may be Jesus himself.

25. The episode of the palm tree is for some the *mu'jiza* (miraculous sign) which qualifies Mary as a prophet.

27-8. Accusations of unchastity against Mary are not reported in the Gospels, but their likelihood is implied by Matthew 1.19. A story long circulated in the ancient world asserted that Jesus was the illegitimate child of Mary by a Roman soldier called Panthera.[10]

30-33. These verses provide a summary of Islamic Christology, at the same time as they provide a vindication by Jesus of his mother through the establishment of his prophetic status.

30. Jesus is designated as 'servant of God' (*'abd Allāh*), which excludes his sonship, and as a prophet; he brings with him a 'scripture' (*kitāb*), which subsequent Muslim writers identified with an original form of the 'gospel' (*injīl*) uncorrupted by later ecclesiastical modifications.

32. The stress on Jesus' filial piety is also present in Luke's Gospel (Luke 2.51), but the latter also shows a certain distance between Jesus and his mother (Luke 8.19-21).

33. Muslims generally agree that *al-Nisā'* 4.157-9 both excludes the Christian belief that Jesus died on the cross (and was raised) and yet at the same time underlines that he either has died or will die at some point in time. The traditional belief of Muslims is that at the time of the crucifixion God raised Jesus to himself, and he is yet to die; some, however, believe that Jesus has already died at some point in history different to that recorded by the New Testament.[11] The 'raising to life again' is generally taken to refer to Jesus' return (as a Muslim) at the end of time, not to Christian belief in his resurrection.

34. This stricture against Christian belief apparently both points back to verses 30-33 and also looks forward to verse 35.

35. By explicitly denying the divine sonship of Jesus, this verse makes explicit the implication of verse 30.

36. The speaker of this verse is not clear; it may be Muhammad or possibly Jesus himself.

Luke 1.26-38

The description of Mary's annunciation forms a key part of the birth narratives with which Luke prefaces his Gospel. It follows the account (1.5-25) of another visit by the angel Gabriel, leading to the conception of John the Baptist by Mary's cousin Elizabeth, and leads into the story (1.39-56) of the meeting of the two women at which Mary utters her ecstatic hymn of praise. This whole sequence of events is a sign of the revival of the prophetic Spirit of God in Israel, but the events of 1.26-38 cannot adequately be described in terms of prophecy alone. While these verses, and Mary's decisive role within them, are rooted in the imagery and the faith of the Hebrew scriptures, they also signal for Christians the beginning of a decisively new way in which God chooses to relate to his people.

Biblical text

> [26]In the sixth month the angel Gabriel was sent by God to a
> town in Galilee called Nazareth, [27]to a virgin engaged to a man
> whose name was Joseph, of the house of David. The virgin's
> name was Mary. [28]And he came to her and said, 'Greetings,
> favoured one! The Lord is with you.' [29]But she was much per-
> plexed by his words and pondered what sort of greeting this
> might be. [30]The angel said to her, 'Do not be afraid, Mary, for
> you have found favour with God. [31]And now, you will conceive
> in your womb and bear a son, and you will name him Jesus. [32]He
> will be great, and will be called the Son of the Most High, and
> the Lord God will give to him the throne of his ancestor David.
> [33]He will reign over the house of Jacob forever, and of his
> kingdom there will be no end.' [34]Mary said to the angel, 'How
> can this be, since I am a virgin?' [35]The angel said to her, 'The
> Holy Spirit will come upon you, and the power of the Most High
> will overshadow you; therefore the child to be born will be holy;
> he will be called Son of God. [36]And now, your relative Elizabeth
> in her old age has also conceived a son; and this is the sixth
> month for her who was said to be barren. [37]For nothing will be
> impossible with God.' [38]Then Mary said, 'Here am I, the servant
> of the Lord; let it be with me according to your word.' Then the
> angel departed from her.

Commentary

This is one of the best-known passages in the Gospels, and has served as one of the richest sources of inspiration for Christian art and devotion through the ages. Images of the annunciation show Mary seated either reading or spinning,[12] a young woman encountering her angelic visitor with the presence of the Spirit also often symbolized. The careful detail of such pictures powerfully expresses the specificity of the human context which this narrative records as the point at which the divine takes birth within the world. The text makes clear that this is an event located at a particular time and place, and carried forward through the agency of named individuals. Moreover, the allusions to the Hebrew scriptures, and to the Davidic genealogy of Joseph and Jesus, give a sense of historical depth to Mary's immediate setting by inserting her within the long history of God's dealings with his people Israel: Mary in Christian understanding in some ways serves as a bridge between the two covenants. Despite Mary's evident prominence, though, the purpose of the text is not to point to her in herself, but to interpret her role in the conception of Jesus: its emphasis is Christological throughout.

Thus, the pivotal point of the passage lies in Mary's freely given assent, the *fiat mihi* with which she finally answers the angel (38). The scripture builds up to this 'punch line' by developing a dialogue between the virgin and her supernatural visitor in which her trust and confidence are gradually built up; once her answer is given, Gabriel's business is done and he immediately leaves. The theological significance of this process of gentle persuasion and willing consent is immense. The very beginning of the incarnation of the Son of God as Jesus of Nazareth, and thus the whole drama of redemption in Christ, is seen to depend on the cooperation of one woman. This in itself shows that in Christian understanding the Christ event has moved beyond the parameters of prophetic experience, for there is no sense of an overpowering or invasive divine message demanding to be expressed. Around the central focus of the annunciation there are indeed other events which do betoken a revived outpouring of the prophetic spirit – the miraculous conception of John, the restoration of Zechariah's speech, Mary's own exultant *Magnificat*. From the perspective of Christian faith, though, these are attendants to the far greater reality of the incarnation.

26-7. These two verses contain six proper names, indicating the specificity of the human context within which the incarnation is to be effected.

26. The 'sixth month' is measured from the beginning of the pregnancy of Mary's cousin Elizabeth (Luke 1.24): the conception of Jesus is part of a sequence of events which convey the stirring of a new divine life in the world.

29. Mary's perplexity at the angel's greeting echoes that of Zechariah earlier in this chapter (Luke 1.12). Her questioning, however, does not lead her into his downright incredulity, nor does she experience the reproof of dumbness with which he is afflicted.

30-33. The angel's message is couched in language drawn from the Hebrew scriptures. In particular, the title 'Son of the Most High' in this context refers back to the promises made to the Davidic line:[13] as Son of God, Jesus is the human figure who will fulfil the Messianic expectations of his people. At the same time, even in this passage the designation of Jesus as son provides an opening to the developed Christology of the Early Church, in which the title denotes his divine status as the Second Person of the Trinity.

32. For 'called' (*klēthēsetai*), see comment on verse 36 below.

34. The virginity of Mary is emphasized to show that Jesus' conception does not spring from any human initiative but solely from the action of God. In structural terms, this can be compared with the teaching that Muhammad was *ummī*, 'unlettered'[14] – the consequence of this being that the Qur'ān could not have sprung from his human imagination, but from God.

35. The language of 'overshadowing' has no connotation of 'entry' or of the invasion of Mary's space in any way. The Spirit provides a protective shelter within which the miracle of virginal conception can take place in Mary's womb.

On 'Son of God', see comment on verses 30-33 above. The Trinitarian allusion seems stronger here because of the proximate reference to the Holy Spirit. It should also be noted that, in contrast to the Islamic conflation of the two figures, Gabriel is here clearly distinguished from the Spirit.

36. Elizabeth was 'said to be', or 'called' (*kaloumenē*) barren. The verb *kaleō*, here and in verse 32 (*klēthēsetai*), has a sense of that which is contrary to the received wisdom of the world, and therefore radically and evidently deliverable only through the direct agency of God, for whom 'nothing is impossible'. It is through the subversive activity of the Spirit that a barren woman conceives, or an unmarried girl's son becomes son of God. This theme of God's overturning of everyday experience will dominate Mary's hymn of praise a few verses later.[15]

38. Mary's response, 'Here am I', echoes the *hinnēnī* formula of the Hebrew scriptures in its expression of an attitude of humble and attentive presence to the divine purpose.[16] Her description of herself as the 'servant of the Lord' (*doulē kuriou*) draws on the language of the Hebrew scriptures,[17] but also resonates with the Qur'ān's description of Jesus as 'servant of God' (*'abd Allāh*) – her acceptance of God's will here could perhaps even be described as an act of *islām* or obedient submission.

The freely willed and expressed character of Mary's *fiat* in assent to the angel's word is of crucial importance for the Christian doctrine of the incarnation, since it stipulates that the fullness of God's saving presence in his world is conditional on the voluntary cooperation of an individual human being.

Scripture dialogue VI

Hebrews 1.1-4; *al-Aḥzāb* 33.40, *al-Mā'ida* 5.3

The texts presented here demonstrate a sense of finality in the Christian view of Jesus and in the Islamic view of Muhammad, enabling and compelling Christians and Muslims alike to speak of 'the end of prophecy'. They do so in very different ways: for Muslims, Muhammad is himself the supreme prophet, while for Christians, Jesus is one who transcends prophetic status. Both agree, though, that henceforth God does not choose subsequently to communicate through prophets as he did before. Yet in that very consensus there is a strenuous disagreement implied: for the two rival claims to universal finality for two different figures cannot evidently be reconciled.

Hebrews 1.1-4

This letter is written to a group of Christians well-versed in the Hebrew scriptures[18] who are experiencing some hardship and discouragement in their journey of faith. It seeks to enthuse and strengthen them by reminding them of their commitment to follow Jesus, linking this with the examples of faith shown by heroic figures from the past. Hebrews develops a high Christology, explicating the significance of Jesus by a religious vocabulary drawn from the priestly and prophetic history of Israel, while pointing to his transcendence of that history's categories. It begins with an elaborate statement of Jesus' work, status and person in which the end of prophecy is signalled.

Biblical text

> 1Long ago God spoke to our ancestors in many and various ways
> by the prophets, 2but in these last days he has spoken to us by a
> Son, whom he appointed heir of all things, through whom he
> also created the worlds. 3He is the reflection of God's glory and
> the exact imprint of God's very being, and he sustains all things
> by his powerful word. When he had made purification for sins,
> he sat down at the right hand of the Majesty on high, 4having
> become as much superior to angels as the name he has inherited
> is more excellent than theirs.

Commentary

Hebrews contains a sustained Christological exposition in which Jesus' significance is developed against three distinct but interrelated backgrounds, all of which are present in these opening verses. First, in relation to the world, and particularly to humanity, Jesus is understood to be the supreme mediating agent of God. He has past, present and future roles assigned to him; he is responsible for the creation, maintenance and re-creation of the world, and for the purification and restoration of humanity. All this implies a functional uniqueness to Jesus' work: there cannot be room for two creative and sustaining agents within the cosmos, nor can the decisive act of redemption be enacted more than once. In this passage, there is thus already evident a strong sense of the finality of Jesus as the one appointed by God to act as his intermediary.

Secondly, bearing in mind that the letter is addressed to believers who are steeped in the Hebrew scriptures, its author explains Jesus' significance by comparing him with other recognized figures who have a part to play in God's dealings with his people. In later chapters, these will include Moses, the high priests and Melchizedek,[19] but in this opening section only two groups are mentioned: 'prophets' and 'angels'. While the latter continue to have a role assigned to them in the Christian dispensation, albeit a subordinate one,[20] it is clear from these verses that prophecy has been definitively superseded by a new and more complete way for God to communicate with his people, through a Son. Jesus is therefore the 'end of prophecy' both in the sense of its *telos*, that to which it points, and also as the occasion of its cessation.

Thirdly, while the images so far mentioned point to a mediating role in relation to creation, the Christology of Hebrews does not hesitate to go a step further in also speaking of the ontological significance of Jesus against the ultimate horizon of his relationship to God the Father. The language used is partly figurative – 'Son'[21] and 'sitting at the right hand' – but it also includes two richly precise definitions of Jesus' person which provide a link between the wisdom traditions of Israel and the developing theology of the Christian Church. The language of incarnation to which this passage approximates clearly assigns Jesus, as embodiment of God's very being within creation, to a status which casts prophecy in a merely preparatory role; it is rendered both inadequate and redundant once God finally chooses to convey the fullness of his Word into the world.

1. The two adverbs *polumerōs* and *polutropōs*[22] can indicate simply a variety of methods and opportunities by which God has communicated through the prophets, but they also carry a suggestion of fragmentary, divided and piecemeal utterances. In contrast to these words, the embodiment of God's Word in Jesus is complete, coherent and conclusive.

1-2. The contrast of 'long ago' and 'these last days' refers to a succession of ages, looking back to protology and forward to eschatology: Jesus is agent of both creation and re-creation.

2. 'Son' is expressive of Jesus' relationship to God as an obedient agent, but the contrast developed in 3.5-6 between the 'son' (Jesus) and the 'servant' (Moses) also points to an ontological superiority of Christ to the earlier prophets.

'The worlds' (*aiōnai* – literally, 'ages') may refer to the succession of two ages, or may be simply a way of indicating the richness of creation.

Jesus is appointed 'heir of all things': all will be gathered together and summed up in him as the Second Adam.

3. The two phrases in the first part of this verse foreshadow the technical language of later Christian theology as they try to express Jesus' status in relation to God.

'Reflection of God's glory' (*apaugasma tēs doxēs*) has a background in speculations on the role of divine Wisdom as an intermediary through whom God creates and guides – in the *Wisdom of Solomon* she is described as 'a pure emanation of the glory of the Almighty . . . a reflection of eternal light'.[23] In later Jewish thought, the divine glory (*shekīna*) dwells among and travels with God's people, just as Jesus does in Hebrews.

The second expression, 'exact imprint of God's very being' (*charactēr tēs hupostaseōs*) also refers to wisdom, but stands at the start of the doctrinal development of Trinitarian thought. The *charactēr* is the stamp or impress on a coin: Jesus perfectly reproduces in the world the essence of God. *Hupostasis* was correspondingly a word which came in patristic writings to have a technical theological meaning, as that which indicates the interrelated, personally subsistent realities of Father, Son and Holy Spirit. In the present context, it has a more general and undeveloped meaning, possibly derived from a Stoic background, of 'underlying reality'.[24]

'Word' in this verse is *rhēma* rather than *logos*; it is an attribute of the Son, rather than a description of the Son as communication from the Father. In a larger sense, that God 'speaks' (*lalēsas*, verse 1) through Jesus implies that he himself is the divine Word.[25]

The epistle will later develop at great length the theme of 'purification for sins', drawing imagery to describe this from the Jewish temple ritual while stressing the sense in which this has been superseded once and for all[26] by Jesus.

'Sitting at the right hand of God' is a figurative way of expressing Jesus' relationship to the Father, balancing the more precise expressions earlier in the verse. It draws on the language of Messianic kingship.[27]

4. From this point on, the argument moves away from the contrast between the Son and the prophets to develop a new distinction between the Son and the angels. This will occupy the rest of the first chapter, deploying a series of prooftexts to establish Jesus' supra-angelic status. This may be in response to a tendency towards angel-worship within the Christian community to which the epistle is addressed.

al-Aḥzāb 33.40

This sūra was delivered around the time when a confederacy (*aḥzāb*) of hostile forces sought to destroy the Muslim community in Medina, culminating in their defeat by the Muslims at the Battle of the Trench (627). Alongside military assault, the Prophet's enemies tried to sow dissent within the community by poisoning attitudes to his family relationships. The sūra thus contains substantial material relating to the Prophet's wives. The verse discussed here is at the end of a passage vindicating his marriage to Zaynab, and includes a powerful statement of Muhammad's status and authority.

Qur'ānic text

> 40Muhammad is not the father of any one of you men; he is God's Messenger and the seal of the prophets: God knows everything.

Commentary

The verse falls into two linked parts: a denial followed by an affirmation. Within its context, the denial of Muhammad's fatherhood of any sons implies an assertion of prophetic authority in a contested case, and the necessity of obedience to that authority as a part of the faith. It is because he is the recipient of God's revelation that Muhammad's rulings are to be followed; indeed, obedience to the Prophet is explicitly aligned with obedience to the divine will.

The affirmation of Muhammad's apostolic status, and more particularly of his finality, then follows. This faces in two directions: retrospectively, relating Muhammad to the line of prophets who have gone before him, as its completion and summation; and prospectively, declaring the closure of the prophetic line from his time onwards. In some sense, this clearly implies a superiority of Muhammad over all earlier prophets, and this precedence is confirmed by the universality of the message that he brings and by the incomparable excellence (*i'jāz*) of the Qur'ān which conveys that message. At the same time, it is essential to Islam that all the divine messengers bring the same truth, and share the same exalted yet purely human status of prophethood. For the community of faith that follows Muhammad, this means, diachronically speaking, that Moses, Jesus and others are seen as genuine prophets of Islam, their messages now vindicated by that of Muhammad. Looking synchronically at the plurality of faiths, it implies that for Muslims the various revealed religions are of equal value in so far as they remain faithful to the prophetic messages which first constituted them.

According to tradition, Muhammad had been the father of three sons, but they had all died in their infancy; this verse refers to his situation at the time of its revelation. Muhammad's marriage to Zaynab bint Jaḥsh[28] was criticized by some, as she had previously been married to Zayd bin Ḥāritha, a freed slave who had been adopted by Muhammad. The Prophet himself had urged the couple to stay together despite their mutual incompatibility (33.37), but he was assured by God that after her divorce her marriage to him was permissible because Zayd was an adopted son, not a blood relation (33.38). A sharp distinction between adopted and born sons is drawn early on in this sūra (33.5), apparently with the intention of changing pre-Islamic Arab practice in this area. The insistence that 'Muhammad is not the father of any one of you men' therefore serves as a specific example, in a contested case, of the general principle that obedience to the recipient of God's revelation is a duty of the faith: 'When God and His Messenger have decided on a matter that concerns them, it is not fitting for any believing man or woman to claim freedom of choice in that matter: whoever disobeys God and His Messenger is far astray' (33.36).

The word *khātam*, 'seal', has been interpreted in two ways.[29] Some see it in relation to the earlier prophets, as the impress on a message which confirms its authenticity: Muhammad's prophetic activity sums up and validates all that has gone before.[30] Others emphasize the seal as that which locks up a container to make further opening impossible: referring to the future, there can be no prophecy after Muhammad.[31] In both cases, the principle of *khātam al-nabiyyīn* is generally taken to imply the finality of Muhammad within the line of prophets.[32]

Within the structure of this verse, it is reasonable to see some connection between the first (negative) and the second (positive) statements: the absence of a direct male line to maintain Muhammad's family raised the question of his succession in an urgent way. Sunni and Shi'ite Muslims came to answer that question differently, but they were in agreement that the prophetic activity of Muhammad was not continued.[33]

al-Mā'ida 5.3

The title of this Madinan sūra refers to a 'feast' or 'table' (*mā'ida*) which Jesus' disciples ask him to send down from heaven.[34] The theme of food is prominent throughout: the sūra includes extensive passages of dietary regulations for Muslims, presented as part of God's revelation to them. It also takes up the theme of earlier revelations to Jews and Christians, criticizing the way these communities corrupted what they received. In the long verse discussed here, these themes come together, leading to an assertion of the finality of the revelation given through Muhammad.

Qur'ānic text

[3]You are forbidden to eat carrion; blood; pig's meat; any animal over which any name other than God's has been invoked; anything strangled, victim of a violent blow or a fall, gored or savaged by a beast of prey, unless you still slaughter it [in the correct manner]; or anything sacrificed on idolatrous altars. You are also forbidden to allot shares [of meat] by drawing marked arrows – a heinous practice – the disbelievers have already lost all hope that you will give up your religion. Do not fear them: fear Me. Today I have perfected your religion for you, completed my blessing upon you, and chosen as your religion *islām*: total devotion to God; but if any of you is forced by hunger to eat forbidden food, with no intention of doing wrong, then God is most forgiving and merciful.

Commentary

The second part of this verse, set in the midst of detailed dietary laws,[35] and following on from mention of the *ḥajj* pilgrimage in Makka, endorses the sense of confidence and assurance which the Muslims knew in the last days of Muhammad's life, after his own native city had been won for Islam.[36] The text is emphatic and comprehensive without displaying any signs of either arrogance or apologetic; it addresses a community whose enemies are no longer to be seriously reckoned with, and which can therefore peacefully turn its whole attention to God.

The affirmation of the completeness and perfection of Islam is made in strong and assured terms. It rests on a conviction of the finality of the prophetic activity of Muhammad, and in itself implies the 'sealing' of prophecy at least in the sense that no further material will be added to the revealed legal corpus which is to bind Muslims. It also unhesitatingly identifies this particular religion, and the community which practises it, as that human response to divine guidance which is the most acceptable to God. At the same time, Islam as a determinate religious system is perfected precisely because it is the fullest definition of the wider sense of *islām* as the universally possible attitude of creaturely submission and devotion to the Creator. In so far as followers of other religions respond faithfully with this attitude of *islām* to the divine guidance which is given them through the revelations made known in their own faiths, it could be argued, they too can justly expect to have a share in the perfection and blessing pronounced by the Qur'ān in this verse.

The dietary prohibitions in the first part of the verse follow on from regulations concerning the *ḥajj* pilgrimage in Makka. The reference to 'idolatrous altars' is probably to stones set up in Makka for sacrifices as part of pre-Islamic pagan worship centred on the *Ka'ba*.

Allotting shares by drawing arrows seems to have been a form of pagan divination in Arabia – a similar practice involving arrows is denounced later in this sūra at verse 90.

There is dispute about the precise date on which the second part of the verse was revealed, though all agree that it was late in the Prophet's life. According to Sunni exegetes,[37] it took place on the day of 'Arafa, the ninth day of the month Dhū'l Ḥijja which marks a special point in the *ḥajj*. Shi'ite tradition, by contrast, associates it with the incident on the eighteenth day of the same month at Ghadīr al-Khumm, where Muhammad publicly designated Ali as his successor.[38] In the Shi'ite view, the act of perfecting the religion of Islam consists in the institution of the imamate as a non-prophetic but infallible succession to Muhammad.

The precise meaning of 'perfection' and 'completion' has been much discussed, though it may not be wise to attempt too fine a distinction between two expressions which appear to be in parallelism to one another. Most commentators refer the concepts in the first place to the corpus of revelation transmitted through Muhammad: it is generally agreed that no law-giving verses were revealed in the Qur'ān subsequent to this verse. Some further maintain that there is a communal dimension also, in that the delivery of this verse marks the fact that the population of Makka was by this point entirely composed of Muslims.

God's 'choice' of this religion implies a definite prioritizing of Islam over all other faiths, not only for the Muslim community but also from a divine perspective.[39] At the same time, the wide scope of meaning of 'religion' (*dīn*) and of *islām* itself should be noted. The former indicates a way of life and community oriented towards God which may be found throughout humanity; the latter can mean not only the specific religion revealed through Muhammad but more generally the humble and obedient orientation of the creature to its Creator which is perfectly expressed in, but not necessarily limited to, the historical system of Islam.[40]

The verse finally returns to the mode of case-by-case regulation in making concessions to those genuinely unable to fulfil its dietary regulations.

Questions from the scriptures

The texts assembled in this chapter lie at the very heartlands of our respective faiths. They speak of the two figures, Jesus and Muhammad, who are central to our understanding of who we are as individuals and communities in relation to God. In some ways they bring us very close to one another in speaking of the finality of God's revelation to us, but they also divide us in describing that finality in very different ways. There is also an apparent imbalance in the relation of the two scriptures to Jesus and Muhammad: whereas the Qur'ān refers clearly to both, only the former is mentioned in the Bible (albeit many Muslims would detect a foretelling of Muhammad in some passages of the New Testament). So we can expect that some of the questions these texts pose will be different for our two communities, while others will challenge us together.

For Muslims, the questions raised by the New Testament witness to Jesus are set against a horizon of Christology already formed by the Qur'ān. Can the faith of Christians in Jesus as Son of God be in any way appreciated within the parameters of Islamic Christology, or must it appear as simply an aberration? Putting to one side the suggestion that the Christian scriptures may in important respects be corrupted, what connections can be made between the depictions of Jesus given in the Qur'ān and in the New Testament? What response can be given from within an Islamic spirituality to the Christian image of Jesus as the suffering agent of God, giving up his life as a freely willed offering for the life of the world?

For Christians, by contrast, the scriptural horizon regarding Muhammad is devoid of markers, and this points to a different set of questions, venturing into a realm almost uncharted except by polemic and apologia. Is it at all possible, given the finality and completeness of that which is revealed by God in the event of Jesus Christ, to recognize a space for any genuinely prophetic event at a later point in time? Is the Qur'ānic denial of Jesus' divinity or sonship capable of interpretation as anything other than an attack on the irreducible basis of Christian faith? What appraisal, short of embracing Islam, can Christians give of Muhammad as one claiming to bear a prophetic message from God?

For Muslims and Christians together, these sharply focused questions raise deeper issues of scriptural interpretation. Can we be hospitable to, appreciative of, one another's scriptures, and one another's interpretations of scriptures, without feeling constrained either wholly to agree with the other or to deny all that the other holds dear? How prepared are we to hand over 'our own' scriptures, particularly those relating to 'our own' Jesus or Muhammad, to the scrutiny and interpretation of the other? Does the differing absoluteness accorded by each of our scriptures to each of these figures necessarily lead to conflict, or could it engender a sense of mutual appreciation and understanding between Christians and Muslims? It is only through the painstaking, at times difficult, but also energizing, experience of reading our scriptures together with one another that these questions can find an answer.

Chapter 7

Reflections from the dialogue

Dialogue is better thought of as a continuing process rather than a specific event. So the 'Building Bridges' dialogue will be carried on not only in any future gatherings but in the ways in which participants reflect on the encounter in their own situation. In the first part of this chapter, Teresa Okure offers a very personal reflection from her own perspective as a Christian, a New Testament scholar, a woman, and an African. In compelling language, she presents a view of the world which is biblical, Christ-centred, Spirit-led, and radically inclusive. My own contribution draws on comments and insights from all the participants during the seminar's discussions. I focus on the vocation to be bearers of the divine Word which pre-eminently belongs to the prophets, yet which in some sense is shared by all whose faith is built on attentive obedience to the message they deliver.

Building bridges: A personal reflection from a Christian

Teresa Okure

The 'Building Bridges' seminar was for me, as for others, truly a heart-transforming experience; it was also a very thought-provoking experience. In this reflection, I wish to share briefly some of the thoughts which the seminar provoked. In doing this I am aware that for a bridge to be solid, it needs to be built simultaneously from both ends so that both parts meet in the middle, which holds the bridge in solid tension. The thoughts shared below are not in any order; I simply express them as they come. If there is something to hold onto or look further into in what I have shared here, well and good. If not, 'there is no problem', as we say in Nigeria. Secondly, my observations are made from a personal Christian biblical standpoint, an attempt to 'account for the hope that is in' me,[1] not as a commentary on other faith traditions. I also share the view that was firmly expressed at the seminar that we first come to grips, *coram deo*, with the contents of our own scriptures before we can effectively dialogue with others about their own scriptures. Further, that we listen respectfully to the radical differences between our books and the concepts we use if we are to engage in meaningful dialogue.

God, the centre of our bridge-building efforts

Figuratively, the middle point of our bridge building is the God in whom we all believe as Christians or Muslims, and towards whom we all tend. A fundamental question for me is this: Is it possible for our knowledge of God, and of God's ways for humanity, based on our scriptures, to be fixed like a signpost when we ourselves are moving and growing God-wards in all other ways in our ever-changing world cultures and historical contexts? Or should we review our knowledge and concept of God as we grow in other ways, trusting in this God to reveal the divine self ever more closely and intimately as we journey towards our fullness, the fullness of our understanding of the divine plan of salvation for us and the entire creation? Is it conceivable that our image of God in the scriptures and God's ways with us can remain ineluctably static while we grow in all other areas of life? In the beginning was God, not us or our scriptures. If in our view our God is not bigger than our scriptures, we may be in serious trouble and bondage to our books. The Christian tradition believes that first was the life, not the book. Jesus charges his Jewish leaders and biblical scholars with poring over the scriptures[2] hoping to find life therein, but they would not come to him to find life – he in whom there is life, he who is the way, the truth and the life. The books themselves are interpretations of lives first lived and of revelations first received from God.

Jesus, God incarnate, God's gospel

The fundamental New Testament teaching about Jesus – a teaching which is not coterminous with Western or even world Christianity – is that Jesus is God's gospel.[3] This gospel is about God becoming a human being for the sake of human beings based on God's incomprehensible and unfathomable, mysterious love for human beings. This teaching, therefore, is not about human beings becoming divinized. Without grasping this fundamental message about God's action and salvation in Jesus of Nazareth, one cannot hope to understand the Christian religion revealed in the New Testament. This message permeates every New Testament work. So the question that was raised at the seminar about the need to identify the fundamental beliefs and differences of our different religions and scriptures remains a sine qua non for effective dialogue. In the testimony of these New Testament works the belief in an Incarnate God was not and could not have been reasoned out from the Jewish religion with its strong sense of election and faith in monotheism. The New

Testament witnesses are unanimous that this message, with its resulting inclusion of the Gentiles, was quite contrary to what they themselves had been brought up in and held as coming from God.[4] So they held, believed and transmitted the gospel message as divine revelation, which they themselves had to grapple with to believe.

Jesus' resurrection from the dead, which he predicted, and Pentecost, the coming of God's Holy Spirit which Jesus promised and eventually sent to help the apostles understand his person and mission, constitute events which led them into the complete truth about God's presence in Jesus and God's plans and purposes to reconcile to the divine self in him the whole of humanity and the entire creation.[5] Their belief that there is no other name under heaven by which we may be saved[6] or that there is only one mediator between God and human beings, is based on this belief that in Jesus of Nazareth, God is personally present and active.[7] All that any human being can do in the face of this mystery of incredible love is to accept it in faith or to reject it based on human reasoning and arguments (*ad hominem*). But our believing or not believing adds and changes nothing to what God has done. Scripture holds that God did not consult or ask the permission of any human being to make and accomplish this plan of salvation in Christ.[8] So God cannot depend on human beings for its authenticity, validation, effectiveness or nullity.

This, for me, is crucial. Often one hears that people of other faiths, and even some Christians, do not believe in the divinity of Jesus. One also gets the impression that because they do not believe, Jesus' divinity thereby becomes null and void. Could anything be more absurd? Human beings cannot dictate for God what God may or may not do, or how God may or may not reveal and communicate the divine self. Human belief or disbelief in this mystery of mysteries adds and subtracts nothing to or from the mystery. At best such disbelief is an index of the inadequacy of human finiteness trying to encompass the infinite. The rejection of Jesus' divinity did not begin today, or in the sixth century. It goes back to the very time of Jesus himself, and constitutes the question at issue in the whole of John's Gospel. It is utmost and laudable self-respect to know one's limit as a creature and to let God be God. Ultimately Jesus' divinity needs to be experienced, according to the New Testament, not discussed and debated upon. Moreover, in the New Testament vision, the emphasis on the divinity of Jesus is more for us human beings than for his sake. To reject Jesus' divinity is ultimately to reject God's own offer to us in Jesus to become divine as God's true sons and daughters. How this can happen is God's doing, not ours. But the offer is real, as many saints have discovered. Because it is a mystery, it can only be received in faith, not in rational knowledge.

The real problem here is that over the ages, we Christians have tried to play God by deciding how God can minister this salvation in and through Christ or God as the sole mediator. The problem is not unrelated to an ecclesiology that saw the Church as an extension of Christ himself, such that unless one was physically in the Church and incorporated into Christ through Christian baptism as a member of the Church, one was sure to be damned. A major point of conflict between Christians and peoples of other faiths lies here. So we Christians have a full responsibility to review our understanding of God's ways with and for everybody, to reread the Gospel inclusively, as the New Testament Christians did, and to review how events in history may have coloured, or even led us to deviate from, the gospel – God's gospel, who is Jesus. In that gospel, the dispensation of God's salvation is not confined to the Catholic, or even the Christian, Church. The Church is only his body; he remains its head as well as the head of the entire creation,[9] and so the Christian Church cannot be synonymous with him. Jesus did not ask Peter, for instance, to build the Church. He said he himself would build his Church (*ekklesia*), on Peter as rock. This *ekklesia* is the drawing of all humanity, all God's scattered children to the divine self through and in Jesus.[10] How God through Jesus does this is ultimately God's decision, not ours. Our duty as Christians is to do just what Jesus commanded us to do, namely, to love one another and the entire humanity exactly as he loved us: unto death and resurrection.[11] If like him we become Eucharist to and in the world, breaking the bread of our lives so that others may eat and have fullness of life,[12] we will indeed be his disciples and we will be able to allow others to remain, if need be, until he comes, should such be his will.[13]

We can thank God that the Holy Spirit continues to be active in these our times in the field of biblical scholarship and ecclesiology, moving us towards a fuller understanding of the person and mission of Jesus, God's good news for the entire humanity, and what it means to be God's Church. We need to revisit how European expansionism, colonialism, Western racism and apartheid, and before that Constantinian imperialism largely co-opted the gospel into the service of empire, thereby distorting the gospel and leading to fundamental 'deviations' from it.[14] Many today are doing a deconstruction and reinterpretation of history. So the question raised by Hebrews remains pertinent for today: are we prepared to hear anew God speaking in these last days to us through his Son Jesus, God in human flesh, like us in all things but sin,[15] in order to free us all from the bondage of sin at the cost of his own life and lead us triumphantly home to that heavenly Jerusalem where every citizen, irrespective of race, class, gender, colour, geographical, cultural and economic location, and perhaps creed, has the dignity of the first-born because each is incorporated in the one who is the Son?[16]

If the Son alone can set us free, we will be free indeed.[17] Conversely, one is also free to choose to remain in slavery or bondage to human reasoning and arguments, thereby cheating oneself of God's free gift of self and of salvation in Jesus.[18] No one has ever seen God except the Son who came down from heaven, the very stamp of God.[19] To enable us to know more fully who God is and how God acts, God the Word became God as human. He revealed and embodied God in a manner that fits our human way of understanding.[20] In Jesus we also discover and live our own vocation to be God in the world, as befits God's true children, loving unto death to give life, and not to destroy life supposedly in God's name.

Criteria for rereading our scriptures

This was a question raised in the seminar, but there was no real opportunity to address it. I feel obliged to identify briefly some criteria with their underlying presuppositions.

The infinity of God and the finiteness of the human

We become aware that God is not coterminous with our scriptures, any more than God is coterminous with the entire creation. Otherwise God would not be God, creator, redeemer and sanctifier[21] of the entire creation. We recognize too that to be human is to be limited. Human beings, limited by time, culture, gender, history, social, geographical, creed and other factors can have only a limited understanding and knowledge of God and God's revelation at any point in time. With regard to prophetic utterance, it may be God who speaks, but it is Amos, Isaiah, Jeremiah, Muhammad who understands and commits to writing what God communicates. Further, other human beings, themselves secondary recipients of this word, preserved them as scripture and interpreted them in their own limited contexts in the course of history. To deny the human and its essentially limited nature in any part of this process of reception and transmission of divine revelation is to deny the obvious. For us Christians, not only is scripture limited and subjective;[22] it is also limited in its history of interpretation or reception over the centuries.

Interpretation is conditioned by the human reality of the interpreter

We recognize that every reception or interpretation is conditioned by the receiver or interpreter. There is, for instance, a male reception and a female reception alongside other receptions, because the male is not the female, nor the female the male. This itself is from God who created humanity as male and female in the divine image and likeness.[23] History has handed down to us mainly male receptions of the divine self-revelations as the norm for all humanity in the different faith traditions. Yet the one who created the human species male and female, thereby positing that the male viewpoint be not synonymous with the female viewpoint, has in these last days, our times, steered us back into efforts to recognize, welcome and celebrate the female viewpoint as an indispensable part of the human reality, essential for our growth into wholeness as human species created in the divine image and likeness and re-created even more wonderfully as one person in Christ.[24] The same applies to the receptions of different generations in history. Examples are the adverse effects of colonization, slavery, apartheid and anti-Semitism on dominant Western biblical scholarship. So the task of rereading the scriptures to keep pace with God's progressive way of leading humanity to fullness in our own times remains imperative, despite the many evils of our age: militarism, capitalism, globalization, terrorism, fundamentalism, exploitation of the earth. Further, in so far as scripture is the record of a life that was first lived, the book itself is an interpretation of how the authors understood this lived life in relation to the God of the Old Testament covenant of love and the God of the New Testament covenant of grace in Jesus.

Each historical epoch is partial and can have only a partial understanding of God's Word

The part cannot become the whole. What past generations did in their own times may be of use for us, but their understanding and reception of the scriptures in their own particular historical contexts and social locations cannot invalidate our own effort to do the same in our own time and locations. It is insufficient, even unjust, to demand of past ages to provide us with answers to questions they never raised, because such were not their concerns. But they give us examples of faith that in Jesus, in the life he lived and the gospel he preached, and most importantly in the gospel he was, we have enough resources to enable us to answer correctly our own questions. Like them, we do this with the help of God's Holy Spirit that Jesus promised to be our abiding guide and teacher,[25] and with faith in Jesus' own promised abiding presence,[26] like the vine sustaining and nourishing its branches.[27]

Belief in God's abiding and ever active presence in our human history

This follows from all that has been said so far. The God who spoke to peoples in the past continues to speak to us today in the evolution of human history. The events of our times challenge us to listen with ears to the ground and hear God speaking to us today through these world situations and the scriptures, in new ways. By so doing we gain new insights into the scriptures and realize that we cannot restrict God's active presence only to past interpretations. To dare to hear afresh God's good news in our own times requires the faith, courage and freedom of God's children. In so doing we overcome a possible fear that rediscovering the fuller truth of the scriptures might call us to radical conversion as it did the Israelites of old when they discovered the Book of the Law in the time of King Josiah. Yet perfect love drives out fear. When God in Christ freed us, God really intended us to be free.[28]

The Holy Spirit leads into the complete truth

At one point in the seminar discussions, I sensed that I had touched a nerve centre in our differences when I mentioned that Jesus promised to send us the Holy Spirit to lead us into the complete truth. I am aware that in the Qur'ān Jesus foretells the coming of Muhammad and that Muslims believe that Muhammad is the 'Paraclete' promised by Jesus, but my belief in Jesus' promise is not located in the Qur'ān. The very disciples who recorded that Jesus promised to send them the Holy Spirit also recorded that he gave them specific instructions on where to wait to receive this Holy Spirit;[29] they did receive this Holy Spirit, which led and guided every step of the Church's mission. A latecomer like Paul, born when nobody expected it,[30] lived and breathed his entire Christian life in the Holy Spirit.

In the Lukan schema, this Holy Spirit came on the day of Pentecost. The apostles saw this Holy Spirit as God's baptism of the earth by fire, the divine energy energizing them, moving them out of their ghettos of the Upper Room and their dwellings in Jerusalem into communion, to serve as the nucleus of the eschatological community,

God's gathering to the divine self every nation and person under heaven. The Spirit was also imparted at baptism.[31] In the Johannine schema, the Spirit was given programmatically on the cross[32] and imparted to the first disciples on the day of the resurrection.[33]

Further, the same disciples record that this Holy Spirit transformed them radically from fearful, timid, runaway disciples into bold and fearless disciples, able to confront their highest religious authorities and rejoice that they were found worthy to suffer for the Name (whereas before their designated leader would not even want to be identified with Jesus before a mere maid doorkeeper). They believed that the Holy Spirit gave them new birth or made them sons and daughters of God,[34] even heirs of God and co-heirs with Christ.[35] Besides, in New Testament faith, this Holy Spirit is offered free of charge to every person.

The Holy Spirit promised by Jesus is one, not a split personality, and has a very clearly defined identity and mission: comforter, teacher, counsellor, the Spirit of truth leading the disciples to the complete truth, helping them to understand and recall all that Jesus had taught and said to them, and to gain new insights into his teaching. The Spirit was sent in Jesus' own name to 'glorify' him,[36] not to deny or contradict him. The Spirit was divine in nature, not a creature divinized, God's own life principle or breath, energizing persons and the entire creation, leading to their God-intended fullness. Romans 8 has a heart-warming and heart-transforming proclamation of the place of the Holy Spirit in the life of the individual and of the entire creation.

Therefore, if later in history another Holy Spirit arises, totally different from the one Jesus promised, that Holy Spirit cannot be equated with the one mentioned in the Christian scriptures. God does not speak in a double tongue, and cannot contradict the divine self. Faithfulness to the Christian scriptures allows of no other interpretation or understanding of the Holy Spirit. The early Christians did not invent the Holy Spirit. They experienced her as God's gift to them. This gift, like the incarnation itself, was solely for our own human good, not for God's good, that of Jesus or that of the Spirit.

When as a Christian I recall that Jesus promised to send the Holy Spirit to lead his disciples into the complete truth, I am speaking within the truth of the Christian scripture, not within that of another revelation. In this area, too, we need to come to grips with our fundamental differences if we are to engage in any fruitful and liberating dialogue. Is it possible for this truth of the Christian scripture to be invalidated by another claim that comes some six hundred years later? What Paul says of the Torah may apply here: the law which came four hundred and thirty years later cannot invalidate or annul God's promise to Abraham, that in him all the families of the earth will be blessed or will bless themselves, and that this, being a divine promise, was not and could not have been merited.[37] Consequently, it could and can still only be received by faith. Besides, a Christian who has not experienced the energizing power and action of God's Holy Spirit in his or her daily life, has not yet woken up to his or her unsurpassable dignity as God's child, or to the fact that God has poured into their hearts this Holy Spirit who will indwell them, enable them to call God 'Daddy', 'Abba, Father',[38] and pray to God for them when they run out of words and knowledge of how to pray.[39] In sum, without the Holy Spirit it is impossible to be a Christian or to relate to Jesus.[40]

The prayerful search continues for meaning, for new eyes for reading and new ears for hearing God, in life and in the scriptures. May God's Holy Spirit make us ready and willing to be led progressively to the complete truth.

Amen.[41]

Bearing the Word: Prophecy in Christian and Islamic scriptures

Michael Ipgrave

In this final essay, I seek to draw together and reflect on some of the themes which emerged during discussions in the seminar. The material is loosely organized around three themes: the prophet's encounter with God; his relationship with his people; and the place in prophetic religion of Jesus and Muhammad.

God and his prophets

Criteria for prophethood

The most important question raised by any claimant to speak as a prophet is that of authenticity: is the message which he delivers truly from God, or does it have its origins in some other source, whether another spiritual power or the prophet's own imagination? In ancient Israel, there is a continuing struggle to discern true prophets from false; several biblical passages give evidence or even examples of the latter. Compiled over a long period of time, the Hebrew scriptures record not only the delivery of prophetic messages but also their outworking within subsequent history, and in some cases their reinterpretation or recalibration in the light of that history. This is not to suggest that Hebrew prophecy should be seen primarily as a predictive phenomenon; the prefix carries more the implication of 'forth-telling' than 'fore-telling'. However, it does mean that the most important test applied to any prophecy is that of outcome: if the word delivered in some sense 'comes true', then it is shown to have been a genuine communication from God, and the prophet's integrity is vindicated. A subsequent development of this criterion arises in the light both of the catastrophic events of Israel's history and of the faithlessness which, according to prophetic theology, gave rise to disaster: namely, that true prophecy sets out a harsh and realistic view of the situation facing the people, as contrasted with the easy security offered by impostors. Even those charged with the awesome responsibility of delivering a message from God are not immune from the possibility of moral fault or self-deception: the Hebrew scriptures at several points criticize individual prophets more or less severely.

The context of the Qur'ān is rather different, though here too the concern to authenticate prophecy is paramount. Muhammad in his own context, particularly in Makka, was faced with the challenge that his utterances were not divine revelations but rather the human compositions of a poet. The Qur'ān responds to this accusation by pointing to the self-validating inimitability of its own text, but also by drawing attention to a sequence of figures from history who are to be acknowledged as messengers from God. This is an *a posteriori* perspective: by aligning Muhammad with these prophets who faced persecution in the past, it validates him as he faces persecution in the present. This in turn implies two further criteriological principles for prophecy. One is that of consistency: the lifestyle of all members in the sequence must be uniform, and what they preach must be identical. The other is that of a preservation from sin and error extended to the prophets so that they can faithfully deliver the divine message, so that impeccability and infallibility thus become distinctive marks in Islamic 'prophetology' (*nubuwwat*).

The activity of prophets in the Christian Church is also to be noted. In this situation, the theological parameters state that the fullness of saving revelation has already been delivered in the person and work of Jesus. There is in principle nothing further that a new message could add to this, but Jesus' own promise of the Holy Spirit pointed to a continuing sense that divine guidance would be provided for his disciples. The Christian community thus developed a series of criteria for testing spirits, which included the intelligibility of prophetic utterances, their usefulness for edification, and, centrally, their consonance with the confession of the Church's faith. In this process of discernment and reception, the prophets came to be clearly and emphatically subordinated to apostolic leadership. Those who most fully display in Christianity a sense of being 'sent' with divine authority are no longer prophets charged with the Word of God but heralds of a new life flowing from the risen Jesus.

Receiving the Word

Bible and Qur'ān alike insist that the divine Word in prophecy comes from the beyond, transcendent in its origin, unconstrained in its delivery, and absolute in its imperative. Certainly a prophetic word in the Hebrew scriptures will be addressed to a particular historical situation, and the Qur'ānic message is to be interpreted by reference to the 'occasions' of revelation (*asbāb al-nuzūl*) within which it is delivered. Yet in neither case is there any sense that the created context is causative of prophecy; the otherness and freedom of the divine Word require and ensure that its origin lies wholly within the disposal of the divine initiative.

The scriptures, though, also speak of that alterity finding its expression through the human figure of the prophet, and it is to be expected that such a momentous happening will have a transforming effect on the created receptacle appointed for its enactment. Both Bible and Qur'ān trace various patterns of behaviour which mark the prophet's reception of the Word. There are suggestions of an element of preparation prior to the revelatory event; this may be manifest as the prophet's own engagement in religious activities (retreat, meditation, *taḥannuth*), but it may also presuppose God's own selection and making ready of the prophet, reaching back even to generations before his birth. There may also be time for a process that might be described as 'sedimentation', when the Word has the opportunity to settle into the prophet's soul or mind, before it is presented to his audience – the human preparation for prophetic activity according to this pattern follows after the divine encounter which has initiated it. In either case, the prophet is marked out as in some way different from his fellows; while remaining with them entirely a human creature before his Creator, the immediacy with which the divine has invaded his personality cannot leave him unaffected.

There is thus inherent in the prophetic experience a more or less violent sense of rupture. To whatever tenuous degree a sense of prior preparation or of subsequent sedimentation may create a link across time, it remains true that the prophet's biography is divided into two halves by the encounter with transcendence. The rupture changes the way he sees himself in relation to the ancestors who have gone before him; the past is opened up to the scrutiny of the God who calls from the end waiting beyond historical time, and needs to be revisioned in that light. The rupture applies with urgent force to the web of relations binding the prophet to his own society. The summons of the God who requires justice and obedience isolates his messenger from the corruption around him, so that he is led to seek his identity in a new community oriented to the divine. The sense of pervasive discontinuity even enters into the prophet's inner self, bringing him a brokenness and pain out of which he turns for reassurance to the God whose Word has brought him into this crisis. Yet both traditions also see this crisis as the beginning of a transformation which will remake the prophet himself, and which, through him, is offered to the community of those who follow his message.

Intimacy and respect

The very possibility of prophecy in Judaism, Christianity and Islam is premised upon an awareness of the proximity of God to all his creation, and a detailed divine knowledge of human thought and speech in particular. When the prophetic event is realized, this epistemological nearness translates into a flow of communicative immediacy, at least in the direction from Creator to creature. Hebrew, Christian and Islamic accounts of the divine–human relationship differ in their view of the extent to which a bond of mutuality can be developed, even though in all three theologies the distinctiveness of the prophetic experience already implies some kind of a special presence of the prophet towards God.

In the Hebrew scriptures, the prophets are shown engaged in a dialogue with the God of Israel that is at times startlingly free in its conduct. The servants of God confide in him, bargain with him, complain to him, express their disillusionment with him, even reprove him in ways which betoken a growing sense of confidence in their rights as prophets to do so. None of this diminishes the ontological gap between divine and human, nor does it lessen the worship due from the creature to the Creator, but it does express a powerful sense of personal intimacy with God. In some parts of the prophetic history, the sense of intimacy is accentuated by the messengers' experience of alienation from their immediate context; in other phases, particularly after the exile, there seems to be something of a 'democratization' of intimacy, with all Israel to be collectively conscious of themselves as God's beloved child.

In a Christian reading of the Hebrew prophets, this intimacy is identified as a typology of the relationship of Father and Son. Like any typological reading, this carries the double sense of both foreshadowing and being superseded. The closeness of Jesus' communion with the God he called Abba, 'Father', and the confidence with which he addresses him throughout the Gospels, brings into his present the immediacy of the prophetic–divine relationships of the past. On the other hand, Jesus is the Son who from eternity has been 'in the bosom' of the Father, the one who as no other human has 'seen God', and in that sense surpasses even Moses.[42] The New Testament then extends this immediate and lasting access to all who are identified with Jesus, asserting that his disciples are made children and friends of God, and as such brought closer than servants. Yet, even as this promise is made, there is continuing emphasis on the importance of discipline in reaching and maintaining such intimacy: those who love God are those who do his will.[43]

Islamic spirituality is considerably more circumspect in speaking about the possibility of intimacy with God. In the prophetic experience, as also in the Sufi project of drawing close to God, comportment must remain in line with the requirements of *adab*, the code of etiquette, courtesy or good manners which applies in a given situation. In the case of divine–human relationships, *adab* will involve behaving as if one is in the presence of a monarch, always being conscious of the difference between lordship and servanthood, maintaining proper limits, and avoiding any disrespect. This does not itself rule out a sense of intimacy, as *adab* in any context is that behaviour which facilitates genuine meeting and conversation. However, closeness to the divine will be expressed within a framework of propriety which excludes some of the elements of informality and mutuality in the Hebrew prophets' dialogue with God.

Genealogy and universality

The identity and character of the God who reveals himself through prophetic activity is disclosed in relation to the audience for the prophetic message. Throughout the Hebrew scriptures, even in those passages where his universal dominion and sole reality are most unambiguously declared, the God who speaks through the prophets to Israel is identified as the God of Israel, bound to them in a covenant which guarantees his special care for them. Repeatedly, this identification is given a historical depth by providing this God with a genealogy; he is the One who appeared to the patriarchs, and the One who brought Israel out of Egypt. Disclosure of this God cannot in the Bible be separated from the calling and the experience of this people, even when their unfolding destiny is seen to be a vocation for the enlightenment of all the nations. The universal impetus of this story, and the universally accessible identity of God, are made still more explicit within the Christian dispensation, but the New Testament, like the Church following it, is still resolute in maintaining the privileged position of this one genealogy within the history of God.

The Qur'ān also makes appeal to the sequence of messengers divinely sent throughout history, but these are no longer in principle bound to one people: even among those identified by name are some not included within the biblical record, while elsewhere every nation can claim to have received its own prophetic visitation. The God in whose name they speak is, from an Islamic perspective, already the universal, eternal and uniquely existent divinity to whose activity creation itself bears witness when rightly understood. Their prophetic activity therefore has the character of reminding humans of a truth already known to them, recalling them to a path already congenial to them from their primordial nature (*fiṭra*). The spiritual role of the ancestors is correspondingly diminished: attachment to the one God comes not through physical descent from them, but rather through taking heed of their examples – and this is a path open to those born into any human ancestry.

Whether appeal is made to forebears after the flesh or whether believers are inserted into a new genealogy, in either case the prophetic message will necessarily demand of its hearers a rupture with the corruption of the present and its immediately preceding past, even as it seeks to reground faith in the precedents of more distant origins. As history is opened up futurewards to the perspective of the end time, many structures will be destroyed by prophetic reform, many ideas reshaped by prophetic imagination. A potent mark of this discontinuity in both Islam and Christianity is provided by the inauguration of new calendars dating from critically important turning points in the gathering of communities which henceforth understand themselves to be constituted not by physical bonds of genealogy but by spiritual obedience to the universal God.

Prophets and their peoples

The Word that divides

The divine Word delivered through the prophet requires a reply from those who hear it, and typically offers binary alternatives. The purpose of the prophetic preaching is of course to seek assent to its message, which will result in the conversion or reformation of its audience. To those who make this positive response, the prophets are authorized to promise rewards from God – though the delivery of those rewards is not itself within their responsibility. On the other hand, prophetic narratives in both Qur'ān and Bible tell with depressing regularity of those who fail to accept the invitation which God proffers. On the contrary, they culpably ignore the prophecy or actively reject it, in many cases justifying their behaviour by impugning the integrity of the prophet or the authenticity of his message. For those who act in this way, the prophet is charged to announce impending punishment from God – though, again, the realization of such retribution is not for him but for God to enact. Built into the prophetic event, then, is a recognition that it will create division, and in some circumstances may exacerbate disobedience, despite its primary purpose of calling people back to the way of God. So prominent is this reactive dimension that in much of the scriptures the dominant tone of prophecy is better described as admonitory rather than affirmative.

This tension between invariably positive purpose and frequently negative outcome then raises further issues relating to the justice of God which have been debated extensively in Jewish, Christian and Muslim tradition. One in particular may be mentioned, concerning those situations where the scriptures describe a society marked by such overwhelming corruption that wholescale rejection of the divine message ensues, with a resultant threat of total destruction as a punishment ensuing. In terms of the consequences of the prophetic event, the line of division here runs not through a group of people but around them, separating out an entire social context from the continuing life of God's world. The problem arises from an awareness that the line of division in terms of response to the prophetic event may not be drawn with the same encompassing clarity. Most obviously, the prophet himself can be taken to be on God's side in this bifurcation. There are then to be considered his family and immediate associates; those too young to be held culpable; and, beyond these apparent cases of presumed innocence, the possibility of other righteous persons as yet unknown within the society in question.

For Muslims, and Jews, the scriptures themselves, and the theological traditions building on them, seem to offer two ways to a resolution of this problem: first, an argument that indiscriminate destruction can be justified, in the light of God's overarching quest for justice; and second, the provision of a means of escape from catastrophe for a small group, generally centred around the prophet himself. Christian theology has historically woven together these two approaches, insisting both that all can be fairly considered to be under threat and at the same time that the person of Jesus provides a way of salvation for those who attach themselves to him. For all three religions, in so far as the binary model of prophecy is applied to social contexts, there remains a challenge in calibrating an individual scale of responsibility within the collective momentum of divine judgement.

Prophecy and suffering

The rejection of the prophet's message may be destined in due course to bring retributive suffering on the people to whom it is delivered, but more immediately it is likely to result in undeserved suffering for the messenger himself. Hebrew and Islamic scriptures alike record in various ways negative experiences of the prophets which are a direct consequence of their preaching of the divine Word: separation from or ostracism by their people; denigration of character through rumours and slander; false accusations leading to imprisonment or exile; physical persecution, in extreme cases leading even to death. There can be discerned a strand of self-consciousness according to which a contemporary figure understands the opposition and rejection he is encountering in relation to the sequence of prophets in the past who suffered similar experiences. Indeed, in terms of God's successive missions to the world and their repeated rebuffs, both Jesus and Muhammad seem to have sensed that the pattern of confrontation had escalated to a point where their own proclamation was the decisive, and perhaps the final, opportunity for a positive response. In such a situation they themselves could expect to meet an extremity of opposition; while the ways in which they responded to such a situation were very different, it is clear that for both of them it occasioned an inward pain and grief.

Given the frequency of this experience of prophetic suffering, the prominence of its consciousness in the prophetic mind, and the degree to which it is internalized as a component of prophetic identity, it is fair to ask whether it constitutes in some sense part of the essence of what it means to be a prophet. Certainly these experiences are not adventitious to the prophetic vocation, and the Hebrew scriptures suggest that their presence is one of the distinctive marks which separate out an authentic message of God from the easy security offered by pseudo-prophecy. On the other hand, for most Muslims, to identify suffering as a definitional essential of the prophetic act in itself, rather than as an unavoidable accompaniment of its performance, would be to mistake the central theological thrust of the prophetic project, which springs from the intention of God to communicate his purposes to humanity; suffering takes its place within this framework as a test of the prophet's persistence in the face of growing difficulties. While the Shiʿite tradition in particular has developed a rich devotional and ethical corpus of reflection on the undeserved sufferings of the imams, Islam in general has thus not interpreted the elements of suffering in the prophetic witness in terms which became crucial to Christianity, such as expiation, redemption or atonement. At the same time, both Christians and Muslims have recognized that faithful witness to the truth of God, *marturia* or *shahāda*, requires an active endurance that will engender opposition that may even lead to the death of the *martyr* or *shahīd*.

Prophecy and blessing

The source of Hebrew and Islamic prophecy alike is located by the scriptures in the mercy of God. However demanding may appear to be the summons transmitted through the prophecy, and however daunting may seem the consequences announced for failure to comply, the prophetic literature is shot through with reminders of the compassionate and benevolent character of the divine – indeed, it is precisely this active concern of God for his creation which is the generative root of his communication through prophetic activity. In relation to the world, it follows that the prophetic event can itself be described as mercy or a blessing, albeit one which needs to be rightly appropriated in order to receive its benefits. In the first place, such an appropriation will take place through faithfully receiving the prophetic message and obediently following its precepts. In Islam and Christianity, the most reliable paradigm for such a response is to be found in the lives respectively of Muhammad and Jesus, who serve to interpret by their words, actions and relationships the meaning of the divine communication which they convey. Emulation, or (more closely) imitation, of their examples thus becomes for Muslims and

Christians a sure way to make the mercy which God offers the heart of their lives.

While for Christians in particular the symbol of taking up the cross daily to follow Jesus points to the profile which suffering will have in their discipleship, it also leads to a participation in the divine joy which the New Testament describes Jesus as bringing to completion among his friends. The note of prophetic joy is present in parts of the Hebrew experience also, again as an emotion which the prophet is to share with his people. In the Qur'ān, the theme of celebration comes to the Prophet late in the Madinan part of the revelatory corpus, once the triumphant establishment of Islam has been assured; it is coupled there with a reminder to pray for forgiveness.

In both religious traditions, appropriation of the blessing transmitted through the one sent by God has not been restricted in its methods to a faithful response to the divine Word. In Islam, the sense that the Prophet Muhammad's bodily presence was itself blessing, *baraka*, led to a direct quest of the seeking of blessing, *tabarruk*, through contact with the traces of that physical presence. The due limits of *tabarruk* in relation to the Prophet are disputed among Muslims, as is the propriety of extending it to other figures also – for example, members of the Prophet's family, in particular the imams in Shīʿism, or those Sufi saints whose closeness to God is deemed to fill their bodies too with *baraka*. In Christianity, the bodily reality of Jesus plays a much more central role theologically as a result of the doctrine of the incarnation; for most Christians, sharing in some sense in the living reality of his flesh and blood through the Eucharist is a normative route to participation in the promised divine blessing. Perhaps a closer parallel to the physical practice of *tabarruk* is to be found in the veneration of relics of the saints; the propriety of this practice is hotly disputed among Christians, though there are suggestions of the phenomenon as far back as the New Testament itself. In any case, the disputes in both traditions about the appropriate limits of devotion in accessing the special grace communicated by holy figures do not obscure the shared sense among Muslims and Christians that blessing has been made available through prophets, apostles and all sent by the God who acts out of mercy for his world.

Prophetic authority and political power

The prophetic Word is delivered not simply to a people as a mass of individuals, but to a society organized by a system of political power. Moreover, both Hebrew and Islamic prophecies themselves can have clear political implications. The Hebrew prophets frequently address their nation at a time of crisis in its life, calling for the adoption of steps – cultic reform, implementation of justice, collective repentance, and so on – which will bring it closer to the path set out by God in covenant. In the Qur'ān, the messages of the earlier prophets are in important respects directed towards the socio-economic lives of the various communities to whom they are sent. In the case of Muhammad's own prophetic activity, the earlier phase of this in Makka is profoundly critical of many aspects of the pagan mercantile state in whose midst it is delivered, while the later sūras in Medina are in part designed to serve for the establishment of a newly ordered Islamic society. Inevitably, the prophets found that they were engaged in different ways in confrontation with existing centres and patterns of political power, and such conflict was accentuated when those powers were able to call on their own cultic functionaries – some of whom, in Israel at least, themselves bore the designation of 'prophet' – to justify religiously the status quo. In such circumstances, prophecy became locked in a struggle not with secular power but with rival ideologies, each side sustained by a politically charged theology.

To support their case in these contests, the prophets could rely on three kinds of spiritual resources. Most immediately, there was of course the validity of their own message and the integrity of their own vocations. A natural reaction from those currently established in power would be to impugn both of these, and so challenges and defences of this kind take front stage in the pages of the scriptures themselves. In Israel at least, they are aligned with questions of recognized authority to speak in God's name, and the relation of charismatic prophetic individuals on the one hand to organized prophetic institutions on the other hand.

Looking to a broader canvas, the prophets could look to the future for a forthcoming confirmation of their message through catastrophic and punitive events, and at the same time point back to the past to find attested cases of the validation of earlier prophecies through historical occurrences. So again, in the scriptures the analysis of what had happened, and the prediction of what was to happen, in the internal lives and external interactions of Middle Eastern communities becomes an important site for a preaching which is profoundly theological precisely because it is so deeply enmeshed in the actualities of politics and economics.

Thirdly, the prophets in some sense saw themselves as speaking directly to the conscience of those they addressed. Whether through the revelation of *tōrah* in covenant, the messages sent by earlier prophets, or the primordial truth implanted in the *fiṭra* of human nature, that to which they appealed could be described as a set of standards and patterns of behaviour which were already known to their audience. In this sense, despite its at times revolutionary impact, prophecy could politically be described as a conservative force, a calling back to a way which was already established. By contrast, the forces to which it was opposed could be depicted as later declinations from an earlier ideal endorsed by God.

It is natural to ask where prophetic religion is to be found in the world today. In one important sense, for both Christians and Muslims this is no longer a directly available option, since the time of normative prophetic revelation is at an end. In the wider sense of a way of encountering the world in God's name which looks back to the prophets as its paradigmatic sources of inspiration, though, prophetic religion is very much alive today. As prophecy always has, it is likely to entail conflict within the arenas of political and economic life; again as prophecy always has been, it is also susceptible to being misused or even hijacked to justify hatred, oppression and the suppression of dissent. In seeking to formulate and advance authentically prophetic religion in today's world, the same three routes are in principle open to Christians and Muslims: namely, reliance on the revelations granted by God; discernment of the current political process; and an appeal to the inherited wisdom of past ages.

The end of the prophetic project

Contested finalities

The principle, clearly stated in the Qur'ān, that Muhammad is the 'Seal of the prophets' is taken by Muslims to have both a past and a future reference. In one direction, it means that he repeats, sums up and completes the sequence of past prophetic messengers sent by God. Among these are to be numbered many of the prophets mentioned by the Hebrew scriptures and also, in a place of particular esteem, Jesus the son of Mary. Conversely, it means that after Muhammad there is neither need nor possibility of further prophetic revelation, since the Qur'ān delivered through him is the full and final statement of God's communication to humanity. This does not, of course, mean that theological activity in Islam has no place after Muhammad; but rather that such activity is restricted to the interpretation, clarification and application of a revelation that has already been made. It is indeed held that these processes are under divine guidance, yet since the death of the Prophet they cannot be described as 'prophecy'.

For Christians, Jesus also marks a decisive turning-point in the history of prophecy as a divinely initiated dialogue with the world. The New Testament weaves together several different interpretative languages from the Hebrew scriptures to point to his significance, and one of the most important of these strands is certainly the prophetic. Jesus probably saw himself, and was certainly seen by his disciples, as standing at the culmination of the line of messengers sent by God to Israel. Christian faith also insists that Jesus is more than a prophet; cross and resurrection establish his finality in terms transcending any human category. Again, this means that post-Paschal theological activity has essentially the character of unfolding the fullness of a divine Word that has already been exhaustively displayed in the world; in Christianity, this activity, while clearly human in its performance, is asserted to be under the guidance of the divine Spirit promised by Jesus. There is here no necessary implication of an actual cessation of prophecy, but in Christian understanding prophets in the present age have a much more limited role than those who precede Jesus; there can be no question of their challenging his finality as the One who reveals God perfectly and completely.

There is thus a degree of parallelism in the way that Muslims understand Muhammad, and Christians understand Jesus, as the one who represents a certain term of finality in the divine project of communication with humanity. Although the status of Jesus and Muhammad in relation to prophecy is assessed very differently in the two religions, it is true for both that after these two figures respectively fresh revelation through prophecy will no longer happen. Yet this very consensus as to finality immediately points to major challenges for both Muslims and Christians in engaging with the other's estimation of these normative figures. From an Islamic perspective, Jesus is indeed honoured as a prophet in the line which leads to Muhammad; but the Christian interpretation of him in terms transcending prophecy cannot be obviously integrated into such a framework. For Christians, the challenge is still more acute: as one who appears in history after the final and normative event of Jesus Christ, Muhammad has no evident function to perform, or theological space wherein to perform it, as a bearer of divine revelation. Leaving behind polemic and misrepresentation, can a better appreciation of one another by Muslims and Christians help to address these issues?

Muslims and Jesus

An Islamic reading of the person of Jesus is built into the text of the Qur'ān. This certainly has much in common with what the Gospels record about Jesus' teaching, life and ministry, and like them it relates him to the prior sequence of prophetic messengers sent by God to Israel. Islamic traditions and devotion have elaborated the Qur'ānic verses concerning Jesus into a rich and varied picture of this prophet, and the recognition that this is the Lord whom Christians claim to follow has provided Muslims with a positive foundation on which to build an appreciation of and a respect for Christianity. In this sense, Islam has already developed a profound and reverential Christology, which is generated from within the Qur'ān's own account of the way in which God communicates with humanity. According to this Christology, Jesus' person and work can essentially be defined as those of a prophet, and – as for other prophets – his person and work are finally vindicated by Muhammad's.

The Qur'ān clearly displays an awareness, in both positive and negative terms, of the developed Christian understanding of the person and work of Jesus. Affirmatively, it describes him as 'Word' and 'Spirit' of God, terms which are not used of other prophets. Negatively, the ascription of divine status to Jesus is explicitly repudiated, as is any suggestion of sonship in relation to God, while the apparent denial of Jesus' death by crucifixion immediately eliminates any sacrificial and redemptive interpretation of the cross. These points of difference are well known, and deeply ingrained into the structure of Islamic theology. The question then arises, whether they are so significant as to preclude any Islamic affirmation of Christian Christology. There are different ways of approaching this issue. From a perspective shaped by the horizons of Islamic tradition, the presenting issue will be that of the conformity or otherwise of the Church's Christology to the Qur'ānic witness to the prophet Jesus, which in turn raises the proposition of a subsequent corruption by the Church of the original Christian scriptures. From within the parameters of Christian orthodoxy, by contrast, the apparent resonances on this question between Islam and some of the heresies which afflicted the Early Church can mean that the Qur'ān's position is too easily disparaged or dismissed, without taking into account the very different theological vision of which it forms a part. From the standpoint of modern critical scholarship, recognition of the complexity of early Christological thought, at once notoriously obscure and strenuously contested, can lead to the attitude that any one theory can claim as much, and as little, justification as any other.

As all these ways of asking the question seem to point into inexorably blind alleys, the hope is that honest, informed and respectful dialogue may provide at least a space for a conversation to explore the differences between Christians and Muslims on this issue. Such dialogue will require readiness to think generously on both sides: Muslims must reckon with the reality for Christians of a living faith in Jesus as crucified and risen Son of God, while Christians must understand the serious abhorrence with which Muslims view any compromise of the truth of divine unity, majesty and invincibility. It may well be that the outcome of the dialogue will indeed be that the Christian understanding of Christ is irreducibly incompatible with the Islamic; but at least the reasons for such a difference may be better understood. Such a dialogue, in any case, will have the great advantage of starting from a positive base in the appreciation which Muslims have for Jesus understood Islamically as a prophet of God.

Christians and Muhammad

In contrast to the long history of Muslim esteem for Jesus, seen as an integral dimension of Islamic faith, Christians have rarely developed any appreciation of the person and work of Muhammad; such Christian responses to the Prophet as there have been have, with a few exceptions, been largely negative, and have moreover been peripheral to the central concerns of Christian faith. The reason for such a deficit can be readily grasped: if the life, death and resurrection of Jesus is, as Christians believe, the final declaration of God's revelatory communication, there is an evident difficulty in finding a place for any other revelation subsequent to that event. The problems for Christian theology in the case of Muhammad were exacerbated by two factors. First, the proximity of his mission to the Christian world meant that it could seem that familiar biblical figures – Abraham, the prophets, Mary, Jesus himself – were being appropriated and reshaped to serve a new vision. Second, there were clear and crucial points at which this new message flatly contradicted key tenets of Christian doctrine.

Understandable as the theological pressures were which led to this failure to appraise Muhammad, the resulting imbalance of respect has long been felt to be detrimental to the mutuality and trust which genuine dialogue and cooperation requires. In fact, the situation historically has been far worse than this, because Christian controversialists in the medieval period formulated a tradition of contempt for the Prophet, the influence of which has been depressingly persistent. In some Christian circles even today, it is still common to find people construing all Muhammad's actions according to the worst possible motive, alleging that his prime motivation was a desire for power, and above all insinuating that he was insincere in understanding the Qur'ān to be a gift of divine revelation. There is pressing need for the purification of Christian discourse in this area, to expel the poisonous influence of past polemic, and to recognize the grave offence caused to devout Muslims by such defamation.

Even when that is done, the challenge remains for Christians of formulating an appropriate theological response to Muhammad. This is sometimes expressed as the question: 'Can Christians recognize the prophetic status of Muhammad?' Care needs to be exercised over the language used here, though. It is clear that the understanding of 'prophecy' in general carries different emphases within the Qur'ān and the Bible – and even within the latter, Christian theology approaches the Hebrew prophets very differently to prophecy in the life of the Church. In the specific case of Muhammad, Muslims speak not merely of prophetic status but of one who is the seal of prophecy. It would not be congruent to Christian teaching simply to carry over any of these terms from an Islamic context: if the prophetic status of Muhammad were to be acknowledged by Christians, it would have to be in ways which cohered with a wider understanding of prophethood, and which did not impugn the finality of Jesus. Possible areas for further exploration along these lines have been suggested: for example, to appraise Muhammad according to a model of prophecy from the Hebrew scriptures, or alternatively from the early Christian community. In these two theories, Muhammad's prophetic ministry could be respectively interpreted in Christian terms as pointing 'back' towards the fullness of revelation in Jesus, or unfolding 'forwards' the communication supremely conveyed in Jesus. Whatever be thought of such particular proposals, there is urgent need for Christians to seek a generous and fair appraisal of Muhammad while retaining their commitment to the finality of Jesus.

Bearing the divine Word

For Muslims, divine revelation through prophecy comes to an end when Muhammad, the seal of the prophets, has delivered the entirety of the Word of God in the proclamation of the Qur'ān and the enactment of its precepts. For Christians, divine revelation has reached its end when Jesus, the Son of God who surpasses the prophets, has embodied the entirety of the Word in the living of his life and the dying of his death. But for both Muslims and Christians the completion of revelation marks the gathering of a community around the Word which has been entrusted to them. It is the community's responsibility to apply and interpret the guidance of that message to the situation of their own lives, to commend to others the promises and warnings it conveys, and to enter more and more deeply through its medium into union with the divine source from whose mercy it flows.

This last, inward and Godward, dimension of the life of faith can be denominated in both religions by the motif of 'bearing the Word'. In Islam, 'bearing the Qur'ān' is a task undertaken in imitation of the Prophet, who carried in his heart the entirety of the divine revelation, and was so transformed by that burden that it was said simply that 'his character was the Qur'ān'. Faithful Muslims who so deeply memorize and interiorize the sacred text that it becomes a part of them can be described, like the Qur'ān itself, as a 'mercy' (*raḥma*) for the world. In Christianity, the apostolic life was memorably described by Paul as 'carrying in the body the death of Jesus, so that the life of Jesus may also be made visible in our bodies'. Jesus' life and death is for his disciples the supreme expression of the Word of God; the bearing of that Word in daily life is built on the discipline of a continuous effort to conform the self to the pattern of Jesus, so that the 'mind of Christ' may be formed in the believer. For Muslims and Christians, our mutual recognition of one another as people who bear within ourselves the transforming burden of the divine Word is the surest ground on which to build friendship, trust and cooperation.

Notes

Introduction

1. Previous seminars are recorded in Michael Ipgrave (ed.), *The Road Ahead: A Christian–Muslim Dialogue*, London: Church House Publishing, 2002 [seminar at Lambeth Palace, London, 2002] and Michael Ipgrave (ed.), *Scriptures in Dialogue: Christians and Muslims Studying the Bible and the Qur'ān Together*, London: Church House Publishing, 2004 [seminar at Doha, Qatar, 2003].
2. *The Qur'an: A New Translation by M. A. S. Abdel Haleem*, Oxford: Oxford University Press, 2004.

Chapter 1 What is dialogue?

1. Alasdair Macintyre, *Whose Justice? Which Rationality*, Notre Dame, IN: Notre Dame, 1988.
2. Christopher Morse, *Not Every Spirit: A Dogmatics of Christian Disbelief*, Valley Forge, PA: Trinity Press International, 1994.
3. *al-Baqara* 2.2.
4. *al-Baqara* 2.91, *passim*.
5. *Āl 'Imrān* 3.4; *al-Furqān* 25.1.
6. *Āl 'Imrān* 3.23; *al-Nisā'* 4.105.
7. *al-Baqara* 2.23; *Yūnus* 10.38; *Hūd* 11.13.
8. *Yūnus* 10.32.
9. *al-Nisā'* 4.142-3.
10. *al-Nisā'* 4.145.
11. *al-Baqara* 2.62.
12. *al-Baqara* 2.47-61.
13. See especially *al-Baqara* 2.137 and *Muḥammad* 47.2.
14. *Āl 'Imrān* 3.64.
15. *Āl 'Imrān* 3.60-63,65ff.
16. *Āl 'Imrān* 3.59.
17. *al-Mā'ida* 5.68.
18. *al-Mā'ida* 5.66.
19. Isaiah 1.5-6.
20. Jeremiah 1.9-10.
21. Matthew 9.13.
22. Matthew 10.34-6.
23. Matthew 7.28 says that, when Jesus spoke, 'the crowds were astounded at his teaching, for he taught them as one having authority, and not as their scribes'.
24. *al-Ṣāffāt* 37.84.
25. *al-Shu'arā'* 26.89. This is very similar to the 'clean heart' of Psalm 51.
26. *Sabā'* 34.46.
27. Michael Ipgrave (ed.), *Scriptures in Dialogue: Christians and Muslims Studying the Bible and the Qur'ān Together*, London: Church House Publishing, 2004.
28. Ipgrave, *Scriptures in Dialogue*, p. 134.
29. Joseph Cumming, from whom I have learned a great deal about Islam, has

drawn my attention to the hermeneutical implications for Christian and Muslim reading of scriptures of my own account of the relation between self and the other briefly sketched above and developed in *Exclusion and Embrace: A Theological Exploration of Identity, Otherness, and Reconciliation*, Nashville: Abingdon, 1996. I want to thank him also for offering valuable feedback on an earlier draft of this paper.

30. Ipgrave, *Scriptures in Dialogue*, p. 54.

Chapter 2 Called by God

1. The next chapter in the biblical narrative goes on to give an account of the first two signs alluded to in the Qur'ānic passage, the staff which becomes a snake (Exodus 4.3) and the skin which turns leprously white (Exodus 4.6), and also of the delegation of Aaron as Moses' assistant (Exodus 4.14).
2. *Ṭā Hā* 20.99.
3. This is true of the other Qur'ānic passages relating to Moses' commissioning, with the partial exception of *al-Shu'arā'* 26.10, where Moses says: 'My Lord, I fear they will call me a liar, and I will feel stressed and tongue-tied, so send Aaron too.' Even here, though, it could be argued that Moses is not so much seeking to evade his task as expressing a hesitation over its outcome, and using this to request the additional resource of his brother's eloquence.
4. Literally 'deeds that render others unable to match them', and as such carefully distinguished from the miraculous powers (*karāmāt*) that may be demonstrated by saints. *Mu'jiza* is from the same root as *i'jāz* (see note 6 below).
5. David Marshall draws attention to Richard Bell's suggestion that the punishment narratives associated with rejection of the prophetic message should also be counted as 'signs' (*āyāt*) validating Muhammad's message – *God, Muhammad and the Unbelievers: A Qur'ānic Study*, Richmond: Curzon, 1999, p. 31, n. 13.
6. *I'jāz* was a response to the claim that the Prophet was a 'poet', and the Qur'ān a work of human composition, by challenging its detractors to produce a comparable text, e.g. *al-Ṭūr* 52.33-4: 'If they say, "He has made it up himself" . . . let them produce one like it, if what they say is true', or *Hūd* 11.13: 'If they say, "He has invented it himself," say, "Then produce ten invented sūras like it, and call in whoever you can beside God, if you are truthful." '
7. Ibn Kathīr explains that Moses had a lisp, 'the result of an incident when he was presented a date and a hot coal stone and he placed the coal on his tongue instead of the date. The lisp came from his having inadvertently placed a live coal in his mouth as a child.' – www.tafsir.com, *ad loc.*
8. Cf. *Āl 'Imrān* 3.7 for these 'ambiguous' (*mutashābih*) verses.
9. Muhammad Asad, *The Message of the Qur'ān*, Bristol: Book Foundation, 2003, p. 525 n. 1, cites al-Ṭabarī and al-Zamaksharī in support of this view.
10. For a good discussion of the issue, see Daniel Gimaret, *Les Noms Divins en Islam: Exégèse Lexicographique et Théologique*, Paris: Cerf, 1988: ch. 5, 'La question du Nom suprême'.
11. See further the discussion in an earlier 'Building Bridges' dialogue based on Psalm 19 and *al-Rūm* 30.19-30: Michael Ipgrave (ed.), *Scriptures in Dialogue:*

Christians and Muslims Studying the Bible and the Qur'ān together, London: Church House Publishing, 2004, pp. 43–50.

12. The so-called *Manzilat Hārūn* ('position of Aaron') – cf. the numerous references in Moojan Momen, *An Introduction to Shi'i Islam*, New Haven, CN: Yale, 1985, p. 325, n. 7. See also below on *al-Aḥzāb* 33.40.
13. Cf. the summary of current opinion within the Church of England described in *Sharing One Hope? The Church of England and Christian–Jewish Relations*, London: Church House Publishing, 2001, p. 23.
14. Although it focuses on a later episode in the Moses story (Deuteronomy 32.48-52), this consciousness is perhaps most powerfully and poignantly illustrated by the concluding words of the speech given by Martin Luther King Jr in 1968 in Memphis, Tennessee on the evening before he was assassinated. King declared: 'I just want to do God's will. And He's allowed me to go up to the mountain. And I've looked over. And I've seen the promised land. I may not get there with you. But I want you to know tonight, that we, as a people, will get to the promised land. And I'm happy tonight. I'm not worried about anything. I'm not fearing any man. Mine eyes have seen the glory of the coming of the Lord.'
15. Philo, *Life of Moses*, 12.
16. E.g. Gregory of Nyssa, *Life of Moses*, II.21.
17. Both the repeated divine call and the response of human presence are carried across into the New Testament – e.g. Acts 9.1-22 (discussed below) has these for Saul and Ananias respectively.
18. Knowledge of such a powerful name could also harm the knower – cf. Jacob in Genesis 32.29.
19. For St Thomas Aquinas, the name 'He who is' (*qui est*) is 'the most appropriate name for God' (*maxime proprium nomen Dei*) – *Summa Theologiae* 1a 13, 11.
20. Philo, *Life of Moses*, 14.
21. Islamic theology to some extent has sought to systematize a distinction between 'apostle' or 'messenger' (*rasūl*) and 'prophet' (*nabī*), notably by defining the former as the bringer of a written scripture, yet the boundaries are not watertight – cf. further the paper by Wadad Kadi below.
22. Though not mentioned in this passage, prophets and prophesying appear occasionally in the later chapters of Acts (e.g. Acts 13.1; 19.6; 21.9; 21.10). In Paul's letters, prophesy is recognized as a particular charism within the Church, clearly distinguished from and subordinated to apostolate (1 Corinthians 12.28).
23. E.g. Galatians 1.16; 1 Corinthians 15.8-9; and, trenchantly, 1 Corinthians 9.1 ('Am I not an apostle? Have I not seen Jesus our Lord?').
24. This chapter is in third person form, but, according to Acts, on two other occasions Paul himself gives a first person account in almost the same words as part of his personal *apologia* (Acts 22.6-16; 26.12-18).
25. Note, though, that the text includes no reference to any catechetical instruction of Saul by Ananias – which would have been inconsistent with the claim that 'I did not receive it [the gospel] from a human source, nor was I taught it, but I received it through a revelation of Jesus Christ' (Galatians 1.12).
26. It is interesting to note that the first eleven could also be said to some degree

to have relied for their apostolic status on others in the early Christian community. The Gospels make it clear that the earliest accounts of the resurrection were carried to Peter and the others by the women who had visited the tomb, and for this reason Mary Magdalene in particular has been celebrated as 'equal to the apostles' (*isapostolos*) or even 'apostle to the apostles' (*apostola apostolorum*) – Raymond Brown, 'Roles of Women in the Fourth Gospel', *Theological Studies*, 36 (1975), pp. 688–99.

27. This straightforward proclamation of the speaker's identity provides a striking contrast to the elusive answer given to Moses by God in Exodus 3.14 (cf. above).
28. The use of the definite article confirms that this title should here be interpreted in light of Paul's 'high' Christology in Romans 1.4; Galatians 2.20, etc.
29. Bukhārī, *Ṣaḥīḥ*, 1.3.
30. According to the *Musnad* of Ibn Ḥanbal, 'God made standing at night for prayer obligatory at the beginning of this sūra. So the Messenger of God and his companions stood for an entire year during the night in prayer until their feet swelled' – cited by Ibn Kathīr *ad loc.*, on www.tafsir.com.
31. Bukhārī, *Ṣaḥīḥ*, 1.3.
32. Badr was the decisive battle in 624 which marked a turning-point in the consolidation of the Muslims' power.
33. The possibility of one verse of the Qur'ān abrogating another is for most Muslims demonstrated by texts such as *al-Baqara* 2.106: 'Any revelation We cause to be superseded or forgotten, We replace with something better or similar.' The question, disputed amongst Islamic scholars, as to whether a Qur'ānic verse can be abrogated by the Sunna as well as by another Qur'ānic verse is lucidly discussed in Mohammad Hashim Kamali, *Principles of Islamic Jurisprudence*, Cambridge: Islamic Texts Society, 1991, pp. 158–60.

Chapter 3 What is prophecy?

1. *al-Aḥzāb* 33.7.
2. *Āl 'Imrān* 3.81.
3. *Āl 'Imrān* 3.82.
4. *al-Dukhān* 44.5-6.
5. *Hūd* 11.17; *al-Aḥqāf* 46.12.
6. *al-Naḥl* 16.89.
7. *Maryam* 19.21.
8. *al-Anbiyā'* 21.107.
9. *al-Nisā'* 4.16.
10. *al-Zukhruf* 43.23.
11. *al-Zukhruf* 43.22.
12. *al-Mā'ida* 5.104.
13. *Yā Sīn* 36.6.
14. *al-A'rāf* 7.173.
15. *al-A'rāf* 7.172.
16. *al-A'rāf* 172-3.
17. *al-Isrā'* 17.67, 83; *Ṭā Hā* 20.115; *al-Ḥajj* 22.11; *al-'Ankabūt* 29.65; *al-Rūm* 30.36; *al-Ma'ārij* 70.19-21.

18. *al-Isrā'* 17.11; *al-Anbiyā'* 21.37.
19. *al-Nisā'* 4.28.
20. *Ṭā Hā* 20.115.
21. *al-Ghāshiyya* 88.21.
22. *al-Baqara* 2.58; *al-A'rāf* 7.63,69; *Yūsuf* 12.104; *al-Ḥijr* 15.6,9; *al-Naḥl* 16.44; *al-Anbiyā'* 21.2,24,50,105; *al-Shu'arā'* 26.5; *Yā Sīn* 36.11,69; *Ṣād* 38.8,49,87; *Fuṣṣilat* 41.41; *al-Qalam* 68.52; *al-Takwīr* 81.27.
23. *Ṭā Hā* 20.3; *al-Muzzammil* 73.19; *al-Muddathir* 74.49,54; *al-Insān* 76.29; *'Abasa* 80.11.
24. E.g. *Maryam* 19.51,54; *al-A'rāf* 7.157; *al-Ḥajj* 22.52.
25. Generally: *Āl 'Imrān* 3.33,179; *al-Naḥl* 16.2; *al-Ḥajj* 22.75; *al-Jinn* 72.27; for specific prophets: *al-Baqara* 2.130, *al-Naḥl* 16.121 (Abraham); *al-A'rāf* 7.144, *Ṭā Hā* 20.13,41 (Moses); *Ṭā Hā* 20.122 (Adam); *Yūsuf* 12.6 (Joseph); *al-Qalam* 68.50 (Jonah).
26. *Maryam* 19.58.
27. *al-An'ām* 6.130.
28. *al-Ḥajj* 22.75.
29. *Āl 'Imrān* 3.33-4; *al-An'ām* 6.84-7; *Maryam* 19.58.
30. *al-Mā'ida* 5.20.
31. *Yūsuf* 12.109; *al-Ra'd* 13.38; *Ibrāhīm* 14.10,11; *al-Naḥl* 16.43; *al-Anbiyā'* 21.8; *al-Furqān* 25.7,20.
32. *Āl 'Imrān* 3.79-80; *al-Nisā'* 4.171-2.
33. *al-An'ām* 6.87; *Maryam* 19.58.
34. *al-Baqara* 2.285; *Āl 'Imrān* 3.84; *al-Nisā'* 4.13,64; *al-A'rāf* 7.88; *al-Aḥzāb* 33.39.
35. *Āl 'Imrān* 3.161.
36. E.g. *al-An'ām* 6.85; *Maryam* 19.41,54,56.
37. *Maryam* 19.58.
38. *al-Nisā'* 4.69.
39. *Āl 'Imrān* 3.33; *al-An'ām* 6.83-6.
40. *al-Baqara* 2.285; *Āl 'Imrān* 3.84; *al-Nisā'* 4.150-52.
41. *al-Isrā'* 17.55.
42. *al-Baqara* 2.253.
43. *al-Nisā'* 4.164.
44. *al-Nisā'* 4.125.
45. *al-Nūr* 24.50-52.
46. *al-Aḥzāb* 33.53.
47. *al-Aḥzāb* 33.53.
48. *al-Aḥzāb* 33.53,57.
49. *al-Ḥujurāt* 49.2.
50. *al-Aḥzāb* 33.56.
51. *al-Ṣaff* 61.6.
52. *Āl 'Imrān* 3.81.
53. *al-Aḥzāb* 33.40.
54. E.g. *al-Mā'ida* 5.52; *Yūnus* 10.13,74; *Ibrāhīm* 14.9; *al-Naḥl* 16.44; *Ghāfir* 40.22.
55. E.g. *al-Baqara* 2.87; *Āl 'Imrān* 3.184; *al-Ḥadīd* 57.25; *al-Jinn* 72.26-7.
56. *Āl 'Imrān* 3.49; 13.38; *al-Naḥl* 16.11; *Ghāfir* 40.78.
57. *Āl 'Imrān* 3.49.

58. *al-Nisā'* 4.163-4.
59. *al-Nisā'* 4.164.
60. *al-Baqara* 2.97.
61. *al-Shu'arā'* 26.193.
62. *al-Naḥl* 16.102.
63. *al-Naḥl* 16.2.
64. *al-Shūrā* 42.51.
65. *al-Ṣāffāt* 37.104-5.
66. *al-Isrā'* 17.60; *al-Fatḥ* 48.27.
67. *al-Mā'ida* 5.54.
68. *al-Nisā'* 4.163; *al-Isrā'* 17.55.
69. *al-Mā'ida* 5.46; *al-Hādīd* 57.27.
70. *Ṭā Hā* 20.133 and *al-A'lā* 87.18 (the 'first' or 'old' *ṣuḥuf*); *al-Najm* 53.36 (Moses'); *al-A'lā* 87.19 (Abraham's and Moses').
71. *al-An'ām* 6.93.
72. *al-An'ām* 6.93.
73. *al-An'ām* 6.21
74. *al-A'rāf* 7.20; *Ṭā Hā* 20.120.
75. *al-An'ām* 6.112.
76. *al-Ḥajj* 22.52.
77. *al-An'ām* 6.112.
78. *al-An'ām* 6.112-13.
79. *al-An'ām* 6.114-15.
80. *al-Ḥajj* 22.52.
81. *al-Naḥl* 16.36.
82. *al-Furqān* 25.51.
83. *al-Fāṭir* 35.24.
84. *al-Ra'd* 13.7.
85. *al-A'rāf* 7.158.
86. *al-Baqara* 2.87; *al-Mu'minūn* 23.44.
87. *al-Mā'ida* 5.19.
88. See, e.g., *al-Baqara* 2.87; *Āl 'Imrān* 3.33; *al-Nisā'* 4.163-5; *al-An'ām* 6.83-6.
89. Sūras 12 and 10, respectively.
90. Sūra 21.
91. *Ghāfir* 40.78, 164.
92. *Ibrāhīm* 14.4.
93. *Yūsuf* 12.2; *al-Ra'd* 13.37; *al-Naḥl* 16.103; *Ṭā Hā* 20.113; *al-Shu'arā'* 26.195; *al-Zumar* 39.28; *Fuṣṣilat* 41.3,44; *al-Shūrā* 42.7; *al-Zukhruf* 43.3.
94. *al-A'rāf* 7.65; *Hūd* 11.84; *al-'Ankabūt* 29.36.
95. *al-Anbiyā'* 21.25.
96. *al-Naḥl* 16.36.
97. *Āl 'Imrān* 3.84.
98. *al-Baqara* 2.177,285.
99. *Hūd* 11.85; *al-Shu'arā'* 26.181-3; *al-Ḥadīd* 57.25.
100. *al-Ḥadīd* 57.25.
101. *Āl 'Imrān* 3.84; see also *al-Shūrā* 42.13.
102. *al-Tawba* 9.33; *al-Zumar* 39.3; *al-Fatḥ* 48.28; 61.9.
103. *al-Baqara* 2.193; *al-Anfāl* 8.39; 24.2; *al-Naṣr* 110.2.
104. *Āl 'Imrān* 3.19; *al-Mā'ida* 5.3.

105. *al-Tawba* 9.33; *al-Fatḥ* 48.28; *al-Ṣaff* 61.9.
106. *Āl ʿImrān* 3.85.
107. E.g. *Ibrāhīm* 14.52; *al-Naḥl* 16.35; *al-Nūr* 24.54; *al-ʿAnkabūt* 29.18; *Yā Sīn* 36.17.
108. *Āl ʿImrān* 3.20; *al-Nisāʾ* 4.80; *al-Māʾida* 5.92,99; *al-Naḥl* 16.82; *al-Shūrā* 42.48.
109. *al-Raʿd* 13.40.
110. *al-Māʾida* 5.67 (of Muhammad).
111. *al-Jinn* 72.27-8.
112. *al-Muʾminūn* 23.51.
113. *al-Ghāshiyya* 88.21 – *mudhakkir*.
114. *al-Baqara* 2.58; *al-Aʿrāf* 7.63,69; *Yūsuf* 12.104; *al-Ḥijr* 15.6,9; *al-Naḥl* 16.44; *al-Anbiyāʾ* 21.2,24,50,105; *al-Shuʿarāʾ* 26.5; *Yā Sīn* 36.11,69; *Ṣād* 38.8,49,87; *Fuṣṣilat* 41.41; *al-Qalam* 68.52; *al-Takwīr* 81.27.
115. *Ṭā Hā* 20.3; *al-Muzzammil* 73.19; *al-Muddathir* 74.49,54; *al-Insān* 76.29; *ʿAbasa* 80.11.
116. *al-Baqara* 2.119,213; *al-Nisāʾ* 4.165; *al-Māʾida* 5.19; *al-Anʿām* 6.48; *al-Aʿrāf* 7.188; *Hūd* 11.2; *al-Isrāʾ* 17.105; *al-Kahf* 18.56; *al-Furqān* 25.56; *al-Aḥzāb* 33.45; *Sabāʾ* 34.28; *al-Fāṭir* 35.24; *Fuṣṣilat* 41.4; *al-Fatḥ* 48.8.
117. *al-Baqara* 2.213.
118. *al-Nisāʾ* 4.44,105.
119. *Yūnus* 10.47.
120. *al-Aḥzāb* 33.45; *al-Fatḥ* 48.8.
121. *al-Nisāʾ* 4.41; *al-Aʿrāf* 7.6; *al-Naḥl* 16.84,89.
122. *al-Tawba* 9.84,113-14.
123. *al-Anfāl* 8.90.
124. *al-Anbiyāʾ* 21.5.
125. *al-Muʾminūn* 23.24 (angels, requested from Noah); *al-Furqān* 25.7 (an angel, requested from Muhammad); *al-Isrāʾ* 17.90 (a gushing spring, requested from Muhammad); *Hūd* 11.12 (a treasure or an angel, requested from Muhammad); *Āl ʿImrān* 3.183 (an offering, requested from Muhammad).
126. *Āl ʿImrān* 3.21; *al-Aʿrāf* 7.107-9; *al-Isrāʾ* 17.59; *al-Shuʿarāʾ* 26.31-4.
127. *Hūd* 11. 64-5; *al-Isrāʾ* 17.59.
128. *al-Isrāʾ* 17.59.
129. *al-Anʿām* 6.124.
130. *Āl ʿImrān* 3.184; *al-Anʿām* 6.34; *al-Aʿrāf* 7.66,92; *Hūd* 11.27; *al-Naḥl* 16.113; *al-Ḥajj* 22.42-4; *al-Muʾminūn* 23.44; *al-Fāṭir* 35.4, 25; *Ṣād* 38.14.
131. *al-Shuʿarāʾ* 26.27; *al-Naml* 27.36; *al-Dhāriyāt* 51.52; *al-Ṭūr* 52.29.
132. *al-Shuʿarāʾ* 26.185; *al-Dhāriyāt* 51.52; *al-Ṣaff* 61.6.
133. *al-Ṭūr* 52.29; *al-Ḥāqqa* 69.42.
134. *al-Anbiyāʾ* 21.5; *al-Naml* 27.36; *al-Ṭūr* 52.30; *al-Ḥāqqa* 69.41.
135. *al-Anbiyāʾ* 21.5.
136. *al-Naḥl* 16.24.
137. *al-Anʿām* 6.10; *al-Raʿd* 13.32; *al-Ḥijr* 15.10-11; *al-Anbiyāʾ* 21.41; *Yā Sīn* 36.30; *al-Zukhruf* 43.6.
138. *al-Aʿrāf* 7.85; *Ibrāhīm* 14.13.
139. *Yā Sīn* 36.18.
140. *Yā Sīn* 36.18.

141. *al-An'ām* 6.34.
142. *al-Baqara* 2.87; *Āl 'Imrān* 3.21,181.
143. *Yūsuf* 12.110.
144. *al-An'ām* 6.34; *Ibrāhīm* 14.12.
145. *al-An'ām* 6.34; *Ghāfir* 40.51; *Yūsuf* 12.110.
146. *al-Fāṭir* 35.43 (twice).
147. *al-Ra'd* 13.20-25.
148. Genesis 20.7.
149. Amos 7.14.
150. Amos 3.7.
151. Jeremiah 23.18,22.
152. Isaiah 41.8.
153. In Hebrew and other languages of the ancient Near East, 'love' may designate the mutual political commitment between a suzerain and a vassal, or between two independent rulers, such as Solomon and Hiram of Tyre (1 Kings 5.15).
154. Jeremiah 1.9. Cf. Isaiah 51.16, where this commission and assurance to the prophet is 'democratized' and issued to the whole people Israel.
155. Isaiah 36.14,16.
156. The woman prophet Huldah uses the messenger formula in 2 Kings 22.15,18,19.
157. Ezekiel 24.16-17.
158. Ezekiel 21.11-12, English numeration 21.6-7.
159. Abraham J. Heschel, *The Prophets: An Introduction*, New York: Harper & Row, 1962, I.26. Italics his.
160. Genesis 18.25.
161. 1 Kings 19.9.
162. 1 Kings 19.15.
163. 1 Kings 19.16.
164. Jeremiah 15.18-19.
165. Amos 7.2-3.
166. Amos 7.4-6.
167. Amos 7.8.
168. Jeremiah 1.6; 4.10; 14.13; 32.17; Ezekiel 4.14; 9.8; 11.13; 21.5 (English numeration 20.49).
169. Ezekiel 9.8; cf. 11.13.
170. Ezekiel 22.25.
171. Cf. Ezekiel 13.10.
172. Ezekiel 22.30-31, author's translation.
173. Yochanan Muffs, ' "Who Will Stand in the Breach?" A Study of Prophetic Intercession', in *Love and Joy: Law, Language and Religion in Ancient Israel*, New York: Jewish Theological Seminary, 1992, p. 33.
174. Muffs, *Love and Joy*, p. 34.
175. Exodus 32.11.
176. Exodus 32.12.
177. Cf. Psalm 94.16.
178. *Midrash Tanhuma*, cited by Muffs, *Love and Joy*, p. 33.
179. Psalm 7.12.
180. 'R. Abdimi from Haifa said, "Since the day when the Temple was

destroyed, prophecy has been taken from the prophets and given to the sages" ' (*Talmud Bavli, Baba Bathra* 12a).

181. 1 Kings 19.14.
182. *Yalqut Shim'oni* 2.218, cited by Muffs, *Love and Joy*, p. 36.
183. Matthew 11.9.
184. Matthew 5.11-12; Mark 6.2-6; Luke 4.24; 6.23; 11.42-50; 13.33; etc.
185. Ezekiel 22.30.
186. Luke 23.34.
187. Luke 23.42.

Chapter 4 Sent to humanity

1. The other passage of comparable length concerning this prophet is *Nūḥ* 71.1-28.
2. *Hūd* 11.120.
3. So, e.g., Yusuf Ali, *ad loc.*
4. *Hūd* 11.12.
5. For a Christian reflection on the curtailment of prophetic responsibility, see Kenneth Cragg, *A Certain Sympathy of Scriptures: Biblical and Quranic*, Brighton, Sussex Academic Press, 2004.
6. Genesis 6.5-7.
7. The Qur'ānic Jūdī is probably to be identified with one peak of the biblical Ararat.
8. Most famously, a story describing a great flood is embedded in the Babylonian 'Epic of Gilgamesh' – James B. Pritchard (ed.), *Ancient Near Eastern Texts Relating to the Old Testament*, Princeton, NJ; Princeton University Press, 1970, pp. 23–6.
9. David Marshall, *God, Muhammad and the Unbelievers: A Qur'ānic Study*, Richmond: Curzon, 1999, p. 102, adopts this reading: 'It seems very reasonable to assume that God is indeed describing Noah's intercession as an unrighteous act.'
10. *al-Tawba* 9.114, etc. According to *al-An'ām* 6.74, Abraham's father was called Āzar. Genesis 11.26-32 records his name as Terah.
11. 1 Samuel 4.
12. The penalty for false prophecy was death – Deuteronomy 18.20.
13. Micah 3.12.
14. That theology itself appears to owe much to a later, deuteronomic editing of the book – cf. Ernest Nicholson, *Preaching to the Exiles: A Study of the Prose Tradition in the Book of Jeremiah*, Oxford: Blackwell, 1970.
15. A rather similar pattern can be seen in the narrative of Jeremiah 38, where it is the eunuch Ebed-melech who saves Jeremiah from the miry pit.
16. Jeremiah 1.8; 20.11.
17. Generally known as 'the Deuteronomist' because his editorial hand is also responsible for the present form of the book of Deuteronomy.
18. 1 Kings 22 (Ahab); 2 Kings 9 (Joram and Jezebel).
19. Numbers 27. 8-11; 36.1-12; Leviticus 25.34.
20. 1 Kings 20.43 – *sar w^{e}zā'ēph.*
21. 1 Kings 16.31ff.; Revelation 2.20.
22. Hebrews 13.12.

23. 2 Kings 9.25.
24. 1 Kings 14.10,11.
25. 2 Kings 9.36-7.
26. E.g. Jonah 3.10; Jeremiah 19.7-10.
27. 1 Kings 22.38. The fate of Ahab seems in fact roughly to correspond to the (later) prophecy of verse 24, while the earlier linkage with Naboth announced in verse 19 is deferred for his son Joram.
28. Cf. 1 Kings 22.51 for Ahaziah, and 2 Kings 3.2 for his brother Joram or Jehoram – though even the historian concedes that the latter 'was not like his father or mother' in doing evil.
29. Cf. verse 224. A related claim against which the sūra fights is the suggestion that the Qur'ān is brought down by *jinns* – which would also imply its falsity.
30. As also the preceding verses relating to Noah (105-22).
31. E.g. *al-Mā'ida* 5.2: 'Help one another to do what is right and good' (*taqwa*).
32. al-Ṭabarī remarks: 'The Jews allege that there is no mention of 'Ād or Thamūd, Hūd or Ṣāliḥ in the Torah, but their reputation among the pre-Islamic and Islamic tribes was like the reputation of Abraham's people to him' (cited by Brannon Wheeler, *Prophets in the Quran: An Introduction to the Quran and Muslim Exegesis*, London and New York: Continuum International, 2002, p. 76).
33. A point made repeatedly in the Qur'ān, e.g. *al-Baqara* 2.285; *Āl 'Imrān* 3.84; *al-Nisā'* 4.152.
34. *al-A'rāf* 7.69.
35. *Fuṣṣilat* 41.16; *al-Aḥqāf* 46.24.
36. *al-A'rāf* 7.72; *Hūd* 11.50.
37. Cf. respectively *al-A'rāf* 7.78; *al-Qamar* 54.31 and others; *Fuṣṣilat* 41.17.
38. Cf. *al-A'rāf* 7.85; *Hūd* 11.84. On the debate, see sources cited in Wheeler, *Prophets in the Quran*, p. 152.
39. Exodus 3.1.
40. Both in the *tōrah* (e.g. Leviticus 19.35-6; Deuteronomy 25.13-16) and in the prophets (e.g. Amos 8.5).
41. See also above on *Hūd* 11.32-3.

Chapter 5 Jesus and Muhammad

1. Due to technical problems during the seminar, the recording of Professor Ayoub's presentation was unfortunately lost; the present text has been reconstructed from notes.
2. See further my discussion of this in 'Christian–Muslim Dialogue: Goals and Obstacles', *The Muslim World*, 94/3 (2004), p. 313.
3. *al-Nisā'* 4.171: *rasūl Allāh wa kalimatuhu.*
4 In terms of the statements of John 1.1, Muslims have no problem with the principle that 'the Word was with God', but differ from the assertion that 'the Word was God'. The contrast with a parallel issue within Islam is instructive. The great theological controversy among Muslims over the created or uncreated status of the Qur'ān concerned its relationship, as Word of God, to God himself; no Muslims suggested that the Qur'ān itself was God. Cf. my comments on 'The Word of God in Islam', in Nomikos

Michael Vaporis (ed.), *Orthodox Christians and Muslims*, Brookline, MA: Holy Cross Press, 1989, p. 73.

5. *al-Nisā'* 4.171, *rūḥun minhu*.
6. *Rūḥ-ullāh*.
7. See further below, Scripture Dialogue V on *Maryam* 19.16-36 and Luke 1.26-38.
8. On the important distinction between *walad* (connoting physical sonship) and *ibn* (which can carry a more metaphorical meaning), see my essay 'Jesus the Son of God: A Study of the Terms Ibn and Walad in the Qur'ān and Tafsīr Tradition', in Yvonne Haddad and Wadi Haddad (eds), *Christian–Muslim Encounters*, Gainesville: University of Florida Press, 1995.
9. *Āl 'Imrān* 3.49; *al-Mā'ida* 5.110.
10. For further discussion of this theme, see my essay 'The Miracle of Jesus: Muslim Reflections on the Divine Word', in Robert Berkey and Sarah Edwards (eds), *Christology in Dialogue*, Cleveland, OH: Pilgrim Press, 1993, pp. 221–8.
11. The title *al-masīḥ*, 'Christ' or 'Messiah', appears eleven times in the Qur'ān.
12. On the latter, see further below, Scripture Dialogue VI.
13. Cf. my article 'Nearest in Amity: Christians in the Qur'ān and Contemporary Exegetical Tradition', *Islam and Muslim–Christian Relations*, 8/2 (1997), pp. 145–64.
14. *Āl 'Imrān* 3.54f; *al-Nisā'* 4.156-9.
15. *Maryam* 19.33 – see further below, Scripture Dialogue V.
16. *al-Nisā'* 4.156, *shubbiha lahum*.
17. There are different versions of the text: both in Syriac and Arabic. The Syriac text and its English translation were published by Alphonse Mingana, 'The Apology of Timothy the Patriarch before the Caliph Mahdī', *Bulletin of the John Rylands Library*, 12 (1928), pp. 137–298, and also reprinted in *Woodbrooke Studies*, vol. II, Cambridge: Cambridge University Press, 1928, pp. 1–162. There are two extant published Arabic versions of this dialogue: a shorter and a longer version. The short report is edited and translated into French by Robert Caspar with the title 'Les versions arabes du dialogue entre le catholicos Timothée I et le calife al-Mahdī (II/VIII siécle) "Mohammed a suivi la voie des prophètes" ', *Islamochristiana*, 3 (1977), pp. 107–75. The long version was first published by Louis Cheikho, 'La discussion religieuse entre le calife al-Mahdi et Timothée le catholicos', *Al-Machriq*, 21 (1921), pp. 359–74, 408–18. The same text is also edited and translated into French by Hans Putman in *L'Église et l'Islam sous Timothée I (780-823)*, Beirut, 1986, pp. 7–57, 213–77.
18. Exodus 32.26-7: 'Then Moses stood in the gate of the camp, and said, "Who is on the Lord's side? Come to me!" And all the sons of Levi gathered around him. He said to them, "Thus says the LORD, the God of Israel, 'Put your sword on your side, each of you! Go back and forth from gate to gate throughout the camp, and each of you kill your brother, your friend, and your neighbour.' " '
19. Timothy also rather cannily points out that Muhammad preached about God, his Word and his Spirit. This too qualifies him as prophetic in Timothy's eyes, though his Trinitarian understanding of that formulation would not be accepted by the Islamic tradition.

20. Kenneth Cragg, *Muhammad and the Christian: A Question of Response*, Maryknoll: Orbis, 1984.
21. For a treatment of the understanding of Muhammad in the Muslim tradition, see Annemarie Schimmel, *And Muhammad is His Messenger: The Veneration of the Prophet in Islamic Piety*, Chapel Hill, NC: University of North Carolina Press, 1985; Ali S. Asani and Kamal Abdel-Malek, *Celebrating Muhammad: Images of the Prophet in Popular Muslim Poetry*, Columbia: University of South Carolina Press, 1995.
22. Seyyed Hossein Nasr, *Ideals and Realities of Islam*, London: George Allen and Unwin, 1966; 2nd edn, Unwin Paperbacks, 1979, pp. 43–4.
23. Romans 4.17.
24. *al-Baqara* 2.6; *Yā Sīn* 36.10.

Chapter 6 The completion of prophecy

1. The other major passage is *Āl ʿImrān* 3.33-51, which in some ways complements this passage, notably in its emphasis on Mary's election 'above all women' (3.42). In addition, there are scattered verses throughout the Qur'ān referring to Mary's chastity and her reception of God's spirit in conceiving Jesus.
2. Argued for, notably, by Ibn Ḥazm on the basis that Mary was a recipient of divine revelation, and by ʿAbd al-Jabbār because Mary demonstrated a prophetic 'miracle' (*muʿjiza*).
3. For criticism of an alleged tendency to deify not only Jesus but also Mary, see *al-Mā'ida* 5.116.
4. The *sīra* records that, after Jaʿfar ibn Abī Ṭālib, leader of the Muslim refugees in Ethiopia, had recited sūra *Maryam* and *al-Nisā'* 4.171, the *negus* 'picked up a stick and drew a line on the ground. He looked at it and said, "Between our faith and yours there is a difference no thicker than this line." ' Cf. Ibn Hishām, I, 336f.: Alfred Guillaume (ed.), *The Life of Muhammad*, Lahore: Oxford University Press Pakistan, 1967.
5. *al-Anbiyā'* 21.91; *al-Taḥrīm* 66.12.
6. Luke 1.29-30,34.
7. *al-Anbiyā'* 21.91; *al-Taḥrīm* 66.12.
8. Annemarie Schimmel, *And Muhammad is His Messenger: The Veneration of the Prophet in Islamic Piety*, Chapel Hill, NC: University of North Carolina, 1985, p. 77, refers to the story of the *ḥannāna*, the palm tree which sighed for sorrow when its role as a support for the Prophet was ended by the construction of a permanent pulpit. She quotes the verse of Rūmī: 'Should we then be lower than the sighing palm tree?'
9. A recent exploration is Daniel Madigan, SJ, 'Mary and Muhammad: Bearers of the Word', *Australasian Catholic Record*, 80/4 (October 2003), pp. 417–27.
10. This is an episode in the so-called *Toledōth Yeshu*, preserved in Jewish circles – Morris Goldstein, *Jesus in Jewish Tradition*, New York: Macmillan, 1953. It is also quoted by the pagan philosopher Celsus – cf. Origen, *Contra Celsum*, I.28.
11. Qur'ānic verses cited in support of this view are *Āl ʿImrān* 3.55 and *al-Mā'ida* 5.117. In both, the interpretation turns on the meaning given to the verb *tawaffā* ('take back').

12. Eastern Christian iconography also drew heavily at this point on apocryphal texts like the *Protevangelium of James*, which describes Mary as spinning a purple thread during the angelic visit. In the West, Luke's narrative remained normative; the book which Mary reads is usually Isaiah, open at the prophecy of a virgin birth (Isaiah 7.14).
13. 2 Samuel 7.12-16.
14. *al-A'rāf* 7.157-8. Schimmel writes (*And Muhammad is His Messenger*, p. 72): 'As in Christian dogmatics Mary must be a virgin so that she can immaculately bear the Divine Word to its incarnation, thus Muhammad must be *ummī* so that the "inlibration," the revelation of the Divine Word in the Book, can happen without his own intellectual activity, as an act of pure grace.'
15. *Magnificat anima mea*, Luke 1.46-55.
16. Cf. comments above on Moses (Exodus 3.4) and Ananias (Acts 9.10).
17. Specifically, Hannah (1 Samuel 1.11). The phraseology and spirit of the *Magnificat* in turn show echoes of the Song of Hannah (1 Samuel 2.1-10).
18. Despite the letter's title, it is not clear whether these are in fact believers from a Jewish background or Gentile Christians who are attracted to Jewish customs. The fact that references to Judaism all seem to stem from the Hebrew scriptures rather than from contemporary Jewish practice rather points to the latter. A fairly early date for the letter might be implied by the otherwise surprising absence, in a detailed discussion of cultic practice, of any reference to the destruction of the Temple in 70.
19. Hebrews 3.1-6; 5.1–10.18; 7.1-22 respectively.
20. Hebrews 1.14.
21. 'Son' is used in a predominantly figurative sense in Hebrews (but see also comment on verse 2).
22. The meaning of the two words *polumerōs* and *polutropōs* cannot be sharply separated; their parallel construction indicates virtual synonymy.
23. Wisdom 7.25-6: *aporroia tēs tou pantokratoros doxēs eiliklinēs . . . apaugasma phōtos aidiou.*
24. Harold Attridge, *A Commentary on the Epistle to the Hebrews*, Philadelphia: Fortress, 1989, p. 44.
25. Cf. John 1.1-14. Hebrews' reference to Jesus' role in creation also resonates with John's theology.
26. *Ephapax*, 'once, only once, and once for all' (7.27), is key to Hebrews' account of Jesus' work.
27. Psalm 110.1, interpreted Messianically by Jesus in Matthew 22.44 and applied to himself in Matthew 26.64.
28. This Zaynab is not to be confused with Zaynab bint Khuzayma, a widow later married by Muhammad, nor with the Zaynab who was a daughter of the Prophet and his first wife Khadīja.
29. It is devotionally identified as a physical mark between his shoulders – Schimmel, *And Muhammad is His Messenger*, p. 11.
30. Cf. the tradition reported by Abū Hurayrah: 'To illustrate my position in relation to the prophets before me, imagine there was a man who built a house. He constructed it well and made it beautiful, except for a single brick left missing in a corner. People would go around the house and admire it,

but they would say, "If only that single brick could be put in place." I am that brick and I am the seal of the prophets.'

31. Notably al-Ṭabarī, *Tafsīr* XXII 12. al-Zamaksharī and others face in this regard the problem of Jesus, who is expected to come again at the end of time, but they explain that when he does so he will follow the *sharīʿa* of Muhammad, and thereby testify to Muhammad's finality.
32. The Ahmadiyya movement is therefore judged by most Muslims to be beyond the bounds of Islam, since its account of *khatme nubuwwat* does not interpret this principle in a chronological sense.
33. Despite the high Shiʿite doctrine of the imamate, the *Manzilāt Hārūn* tradition designating Ali as Muhammad's successor specifically rules out prophethood – cf. above on *Ṭā Hā* 20.29.
34. Verses 112-14. There may be references to the Christian Eucharist here.
35. After the specification of illicit foods in verse 3a, verse 4 goes on to explain what is lawful to eat.
36. A tradition states that, on hearing this verse recited, ʿUmar wept because he knew that Muhammad would soon die. Another version explains ʿUmar's weeping by his recognition that, if Islam were perfected on that day, it could only deteriorate from that point onwards.
37. E.g. ibn Kathīr, www.tafsir.com, *ad loc.*
38. Ibn Ḥanbal describes Muhammad's proclamation as follows: 'He took Ali's hand and said: "Of whomsoever I am Lord, then Ali is also his Lord. O God! Be Thou the supporter of whoever supports Ali and the enemy of whoever opposes him" ' – *Musnad*, IV, 281, cited in Momen, *An Introduction to Shiʿi Islam*, New Haven, CN: Yale, 1985, p. 15. The Shiʿite tradition maintains that this episode was introduced by the revelation of *al-Māʾida* 5.67, and concluded with the present verse 3.
39. It may also carry the idea that God is 'satisfied' with the religion as it now stands, and will from this point be introducing neither further revelation nor any abrogation of what is already revealed.
40. The same issue is raised by several other Qurʾānic texts which speak of the choice of Islam / *islām*, e.g. see discussion of *Āl ʿImrān* 3.85 in Ipgrave, *Scriptures in Dialogue*, p. 129.

Chapter 7 Reflections from the dialogue

1. 1 Peter 3.15.
2. John 5.39 – *eraunate tas graphas*.
3. Romans 1.1,16, etc.
4. Cf. Acts 10, Peter's battle with God over the inclusion of the Roman Cornelius and his household.
5. 2 Corinthians 5.16-19.
6. Acts 4.12.
7. John 14.7-11.
8. Romans 11.33-6.
9. Colossians 1.15-20.
10. John 11.52; 12.32; 2 Corinthians 5.16-21.
11. John 13.34-5.
12. John 10.10.

13. Cf. John 21.21-2.
14. The phrase, 'deviations from the gospel' is that of Pope John Paul II in his encyclical *Novo millennio ineunte* (1999).
15. Hebrews 4.15.
16. Hebrews 12.23.
17. John 8.36.
18. Cf. John 3.21.
19. John 1.18; Hebrews 1.
20. Cf. 1 John 1.1-4.
21. In traditional Trinitarian terms: Father, Son and Holy Spirit.
22. I use the word 'subjective' in the most etymological sense of the word: limited by the human subject who received or wrote down the revelation, even if allegedly heard directly from God.
23. Genesis 1.26-7; 5.1-2.
24. Galatians 3.28.
25. John 14.16-17,25; 16.7-10.
26. Matthew 28.20.
27. John 15.1-17.
28. Galatians 5.1.
29. Cf. Luke 24.49; Acts 1.8.
30. 1 Corinthians 15.8.
31. Cf. Acts 19.1-19.
32. John 19.30 – *edoken to pneuma*.
33. John 20.21-2.
34. John 1.12-13; 3.1-21.
35. Romans 8.14-17.
36. John 16.7-10.
37. Galatians 3.17.
38. Galatians 4.6-7; Romans 8.15.
39. Romans 8.26-7.
40. 1 Corinthians 12.3.
41. Some of the ideas presented here are explained at greater length in the following works of mine: *The Johannine Approach to Mission: A Contextual Approach to John 4:1-42* WUNT 2/31, Tübingen: J.C.B. Mohr [Paul Siebeck], 1988; 'John', in William R. Farmer et al. (eds), *The International Bible Commentary: A Catholic and Ecumenical Commentary for the Twenty-First Century*, Collegeville, MN: The Liturgical Press, 1998, pp. 1438–1505; *To Cast Fire Upon the Earth: Bible and Mission Collaborating in Today's Multicultural Global Context*, Pietermaritzburg: Cluster Publications, 2000; ' "I will open my mouth in parables" (Mt 13.35): A Case for a Gospel-Based Biblical Hermeneutics', *New Testament Studies*, 46/3 (2000), pp. 445–63; ' "In him all things hold together": A Missiological Reading of Colossians 1.15-20', *International Review of Mission*, XCI/360 (January 2002), pp. 62-72; 'Colossians', and 'Hebrews: Sacrifice in an African Context', both in Daniel Patte et al. (eds), *Global Bible Commentary*, Nashville: Abingdon Press, 2004, pp. 490–99 and 535–8, respectively.
42. John 1.18.
43. John 15.15.